THE BRUMBACK LIBRARY
OF VAN WERT COUNTY
VAN WERT, OHIO

postmarks, cards and covers

Collecting
Postal History

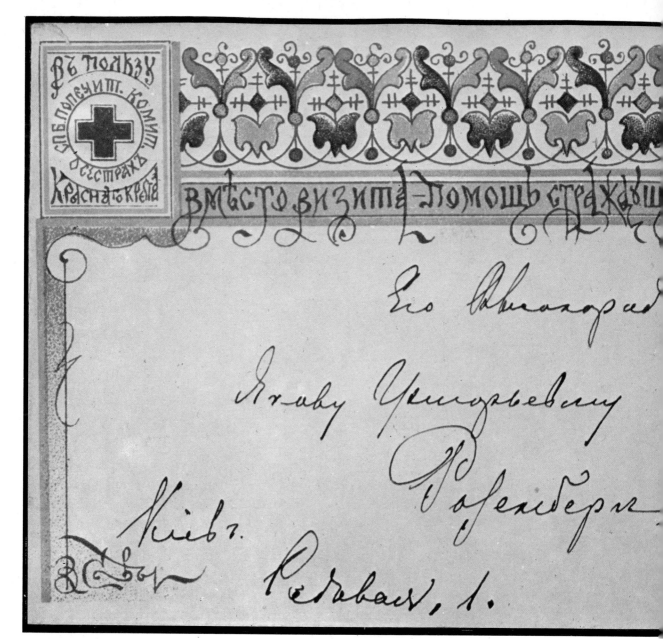

At the end of the nineteenth century, it was the custom in Russian society to exchange formal visits, particularly at Christmas and Easter. To help people with this sometimes tiresome duty, the Red Cross offered to "represent" the visitor with specially printed envelopes in which visiting cards could be delivered. This one, issued by the Comité de St. Petersburg, was used in Kiev in 1900. The printed inscription reads: "Instead of a visit, help the poor".

postmarks, cards and covers

Collecting
Postal History

by Prince Dimitry Kandaouroff

translated and edited by William Finlay

Larousse & Co. Inc.

EDITOR'S NOTE
In designing this book, we have made no
attempt to relate the size at which the
photographs are reproduced to the size
of the original card or envelope. Some
small items have been enlarged to emphasize
their interesting details, while others,
with more clearly visible marks, have been
reduced in size.

Designed by Youé and Spooner Limited

First American edition
published in the U.S. and Canada 1974
by Larousse and Co. Inc., New York, New York.

First published in England by Peter Lowe

ISBN 0 88332 061 4
Library of Congress Catalog Number: 74–78602

Printed in Holland by Smeets Lithographers, Weert

Contents

Introduction 10

1 The posts in ancient times 12

2 Letters, postmarks and stamps 34

3 The post on water 58

4 The post goes faster and faster 78

5 The air posts 96

6 The post in wartime 118

7 Miscellaneous aspects of the posts 150

8 First day covers and maximum cards 174

Collecting covers and cards 183

Index 185

Many medieval guilds maintained their own postal services. This postman wears the livery of the German Corporation of Watermen in the seventeenth century.

Introduction

The story of the post is the story of the development of the most basic means of human communication. Better methods of transportation and the rapid growth of literacy all over the world have accelerated the development of the postal services in the past century, but it is a story which had its tentative beginnings in the mists of antiquity. In this book I have tried to sketch the story, from the clay tablets and papyrus rolls of ancient Assyria and Egypt, up to the airmails of today.

Postal history has, until now, been a relatively neglected aspect of social history. The role of the posts in the socio-economic development of every country has all too often been overlooked. Perhaps we take our posts too much for granted; familiarity breeds contempt. It is only when the postal service vanishes overnight, as it has during postal strikes in recent years, that we become acutely aware of the service and just how much we depend on speedy letter communication in business and everyday life. The handling, sorting, facing, postmarking and distribution of mail nowadays is such a highly complex process that the layman cannot envisage what is involved, and so he tends not to give it a thought. He expects his mail delivered promptly the morning after it has been posted and seldom pauses to wonder at the system which ensures that a letter posted in New Zealand can be in Norway, or England or the U.S.A. three days later.

Space does not permit a detailed account of every facet of the posts, but on the assumption that every picture is worth a thousand words, letters, covers and postcards have been used to illustrate this book. This has been done for two reasons. Firstly, these items illustrate quite graphically, in their postmarks, cachets – and even the mode in which the address is styled – the story of the post at various times in its development. Secondly, these letters, covers and cards are the souvenirs, the mementoes, the historic documents which serve as landmarks in the development of the posts. As such, they are avidly studied and collected. They lend themselves admirably to the role of collector's pieces. They are, for the most part, two-dimensional and therefore easily housed in a folder or album. They can be arranged and mounted as easily as stamps and the pages annotated to draw attention to the interesting postmarks and other salient points.

Postal history collecting, as a hobby, is of recent growth. It has developed from the older hobby of philately – stamp-collecting – which, itself, began little more than a century ago. The early stamp collectors preferred their specimens in mint, or unused, condition, but by the turn of the century a few of them were beginning to appreciate that the cancellation, or postmark, on a stamp could tell them quite a lot about the stamp – its age, its usage, even its authenticity. Gradually the study of postmarks developed as an offshoot from stamps. At first collectors were content to collect postmarks as cut-outs – small rectangles of paper cut from the envelope or card, bearing the postage stamp and its cancellation. Then, just before the Second World War, interest spread backward in time to the period before the invention of adhesive stamps and collectors began studying early letters and covers bearing impressed "stamps" or postal markings. This aspect of the hobby now has a large following and is known variously as pre-adhesive philately (Britain), *vorphilatelie* (Germany) or *eo-philatelie* (France).

The present trend towards ever higher output of adhesive stamps, many of which are designed solely with philatelic sales in mind, is driving the collector away from philately as such. He is turning his attention to the by-ways of the hobby, and that is why the study of postmarks and postal history is booming. In most cases there is no attempt by a postal administration to produce something deliberately for the collector, so the degree of artificiality now present in stamp-collecting is absent. Only in the case of modern first day covers and maximum cards is this artificiality present. On the other hand there is something essentially romantic about old letters and postcards. The messages preserved in them are often incredibly quaint, in other cases refreshingly relevant to the present time. A letter of 1600, in flowery Elizabethan English, from a young man to the father of his girlfriend, for example, illustrates the "generation gap" just as vividly as any communication of today. Of course, a high proportion of the old letters that have survived were written by famous people and recorded historic events, but even the ordinary, day-to-day messages of former times have a peculiar fascination for the collector.

But the story of the post is not concerned only with past events. It is a continuing saga of man's attempts to shrink the world by improving the communication of the written word. Post-codes and electronic sorting are already with us, and have left their mark on covers and cards; and tomorrow we may even witness intercontinental rocket posts. At any rate, each new development in the story will be faithfully recorded by covers and postcards for future generations of collectors to study.

Romas bas-relief, 250 B.C., from the Igeler Saüle, Trier. The
sculpture shows a typical Roman chariot, of the type used by
the *cursus publicus*.

I

The posts in ancient times

To TELL the story of the postal service is to try to write the history of the world, for every civilization in every country has contributed something to its development. The transmission of the orders of the sovereign, the reports received from the four corners of his empire, the despatches of his ambassadors: these are the royal posts. Orders, invoices for merchandise and market intelligence reports: these are the posts of commerce. The health of a loved one, messages of friendship, a pledge of love, promises, hopes or perhaps just news of people at home: these are the posts of mankind.

THE POSTAL SERVICE IN PRE-HISTORY

The earliest examples of posts consist of messages which date from before the birth of writing. There is a reference to "post-boats" in the Book of Job that scholars are still arguing about, but there are other, incontrovertible references in the Bible. In the Book of Nehemiah (II, 7), for example:

"Moreover I said unto the king, if it please the king, let letters be given to the governors beyond the river, that they may convey me over till I come into Judah. And a letter unto Asaph the keeper of the king's forest ... Then I came to the governors beyond the river, and gave them the king's letters."
In the Book of Esther (III, 13):

"And the letters were sent by posts into all the king's provinces to destroy, to kill, and to cause to perish, all Jews ... The posts went out, being hastened by the king's commandment, and the decree was given in Shushan the palace."
Further on, in the same book (VIII, 10–14) we read how couriers carried decrees reversing this decision:

"And he wrote in the King Asahuerus' name, and sealed it with the king's ring, and sent letters by posts on horseback, and riders on mules, camels and young dromedaries."

These references are not the earliest known in history. Proof that letters were sent even earlier appears on the clay tablets discovered towards the end of the last century at Tel el Amarna in Egypt, and also in Cappadocia in Asia Minor.

The earliest known letters are found on clay tablets. This one from Sumer, dates from 2095 B.C.

Below, left: The ancient Egyptians, like the Assyrians, wrote their letters on clay tablets. In this one, the inhabitants of Tunip, near Damascus, ask the King of Egypt for help against a rebel who is threatening their city. They are afraid that he has intercepted some of the twenty other letters they have already written to the king.

A complicated system of sending messages by means of torches was devised by Aeneas in 336 B.C. Though more flexible than simply lighting a bonfire on a hill, the contents of the message were still severely limited.

Between 3000 and 1500 B.C. Cappadocia (now part of modern Turkey) was settled by merchants from Assyria and then became part of the dominions of Ur. Later the area formed part of the Hittite empire. In 1925 the famous Czech archaeologist, Bedrich Hrozny discovered an important cache of these tablets at Kultepe "the hillock of ashes", about 12 miles from Kaisarieh, near Kanesh. They consisted of small plaques of square or rectangular format made of baked clay inserted in clay envelopes. Some envelopes were used for filing documents, and these bore the title of the document inside; others were used for letters, and had an address on the outside and the seal of the sender. Letters like this were sent and received from one part of the empire to another, both by the king and by private individuals. They all end with a polite formula, expressing the hope that the gods would bless the receiver. The messages were written in cuneiform characters and their translation is a highly specialized job, but the letters furnish conclusive proof of the existence of a frequent courier service, and the watchfulness of the state over communications.

Egyptian tablets have confirmed the existence of regular correspondence between the Pharaohs and the princes of Syria (their vassals), and between the kings of Assyria and Babylon. One example that has been found is from the king of the Mitanni (in upper Syria) to Amenophis IV, King of Egypt, and contains his condolences on the death of the latter's father.

The Egyptians had a system of express messengers known as *symmaci* who operated in relays. These couriers travelled in the intricate network of canals throughout the Valley of the Nile, stretched out on narrow punts which they propelled with their feet!

POSTS IN HISTORICAL TIMES

We now arrive at a time a little less ancient, the era of the Persians and, in particular, the reign of the great King Cyrus (539 B.C.). This king is regarded as the founder of the postal relay system. In his *Histories* Herodotus writes:

"Nothing is more expeditious than the method of transmitting messages invented and used by the Persians. Along each route, at regular intervals equal to one day's journey, were relays of men and horses, housed in stations specially set up for the purpose. Snow, rain, cold or darkness could not prevent the messengers carrying on their work with the greatest speed. The first man to arrive passed the despatches to the second, who then passed them on to a third, and so on, until the despatches arrived at their destination. . . . In the Persian language these relays were known as *angareion*."

Some years later the Greek historian Xenophon confirmed this in his *Cyropedia* (VIII, 6):

"Here is another invention of Cyrus, very helpful in the government of his vast empire, as it brought prompt information from every part of his dominions. Stables were set up at intervals equal to the distance which a horse could travel in a day without becoming exhausted; each stable had horses and grooms to look after them. He appointed to each station an intelligent man who would deliver to one courier the letters brought by another; who would provide rest and refreshment for the tired couriers and horses, and who would control the finances. Moreover, night did not hold back the progress of these messengers; a messenger who arrived by day would be replaced by another who would travel by night. They seemed faster than the flight of birds. It is no exaggeration to say that no other men could travel more rapidly across the earth."

The longest postal route in antiquity was one running from Sardis to Susa via Ancyra, Melitene, Arteba and Calonne. It crossed the deserts, linking one oasis with another, was 337 miles long and was marked by 111 stations. A messenger on horseback took five or six days to make the journey, but a traveller on foot took 90 days! Another route was established for the postal service between Persepolis and Susa and a third ran between Persepolis and Ecbatana.

POSTS IN ANCIENT GREECE

The numerous Greek states possessed their own courier systems. Messengers are frequently mentioned by classical Greek authors, but the topography and the fragmented political organization of Greece prevented a large overland network from developing. The system most often referred to is the transmission of optical messages from one island to another. The poet Aeschylus described a simple system used by Agamemnon to announce the sack of Troy:

"From fire to fire the messenger-flame flew thus. From Mount Ida the signal passed to Lemnos; from that isle the summit of Mount Athos received the third signal. The signal provided by a pitch-pine torch had travelled over the surface of the waters and gilded with its glow the post at Macistos. Its light soon alerted the guardians of Messapos on the shores of Euripus; they replied and transmitted the signal by lighting a heap of dried heather which gave out a bright light . . . Thus it reached Mount Cithaeron and continued the succession."

Though this account was written in 458 B.C., the poet was recounting events of a much earlier time, as the siege of Troy is now thought by archaeologists and historians to have taken place around 1180 B.C.

In about 350 B.C., Aeneas, the famous Greek tactician, discovered another telegraphic method. The apparatus was a bronze vase with a hole pierced in its base and a vertical graduated float which dropped as the vase emptied. Each telegraphic station used exactly the same system. The station-master raised a torch and unplugged the vase at the same instant, his opposite number along the line did the same and so on down the line of signal stations. The various gradations corresponded to phrases to be transmitted, and when the float had reached the appropriate level the signaller lowered his torch. Each man did likewise and so the message was transmitted. Although this procedure was somewhat limited it allowed messages to be passed on rapidly and accurately from one part of the country to another.

Much later (about 150 B.C.) the Greek military historian Polybus invented an ingenious system of batteries of torches. There were two rows of torches and different combinations of the numbers of torches in each line stood for a different number or letter. A complete message could be transmitted in this way. But no simple optical apparatus could be seen from very far off, and it is only in modern times, with the discovery of electricity and radio, that a long-range telegraph system has been invented.

THE ROMAN POSTAL SERVICE

Details of the Roman postal system, which developed over a long period, are well known to historians. The Roman road network extended all over the Mediterranean area. It was maintained with great care and constituted a solid basis for postal transport. All along the various routes there were two categories of establishment: the *mansiones* and the *mutationes*. The *mansiones* were important halting-places where one could get board and lodging and vehicle repairs; the *mutationes* were simply relay-stations placed at intervals between the *mansiones*. The remains of many of these stations have been discovered. One, the so-called Villa of Theseus, lies on the road from Tours to Bourges in France. The main room of this building measures 114 by 41 feet and its huge stables accommodated up to 60 post-horses. Most Roman roads had halting-places like this spaced at regular intervals.

The oldest evidence concerning relays is provided by the Goblets of Vicarello or the Apollinaire Vases, four cylindrical vessels of silver, discovered in 1852 north of Rome in an old spa. After being used by the sick to hold mineral water, these vessels were thrown into the spring as an offering to the gods. The goblets

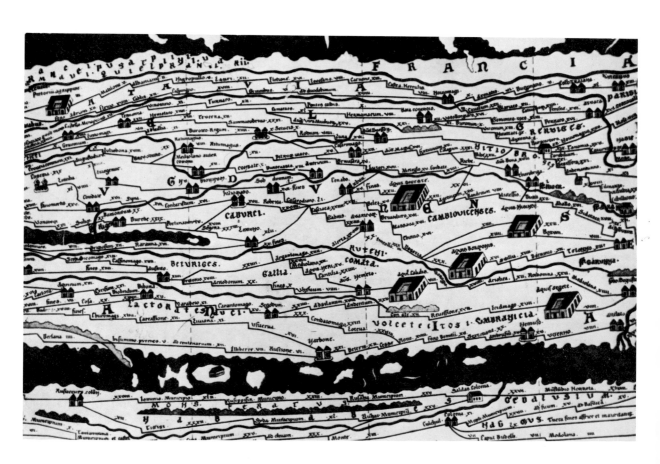

or vases are about ten centimetres high and bear, engraved on their sides in four columns, the names of the stations from Cadiz to Rome. This detailed itinerary gives the relay stations, with the distances between them, and dates from the first or second centuries A.D.

The National Library of Vienna preserves the only known Roman road map. Actually it is thought to be a copy attributed to a monk of Colmar, and probably dates from the latter part of the fourth century. The original on which it is based has long since disappeared. The map, known as the Peutinger Tables, is divided into a number of separate sections. It represents the known world from the Indus to Great Britain and shows the roads, with their stages and distances. The map's scale is curious, foreshortened from north to south and excessively stretched out from east to west. Although it is often inaccurate, the map is of immense interest for the light it sheds on the Roman postal system.

Left: A section of the famous Peutinger Tables, a medieval copy of a Roman map. It shows the Gallo-Roman area, corresponding with modern France and Italy. The post routes and *mansiones* are clearly marked.

The medieval postmen of Hanau were nicknamed *Hennchen* (little hens), because of the civic arms emblazoned on their tunics. These woodcuts, now in the German Postal Museum at Frankfurt am Main, date from 1439.

More information about the system comes from the Itinerary from Bordeaux to Jerusalem (established in A.D. 333, during the reign of Constantine), which made a clear distinction between *mutationes* and *mansiones*. Additional information comes from the very large number of milestones that have been found all over Europe, the Near East and North Africa.

Copies of the regulations for personnel of the Roman posts have been preserved, and these give us an idea of the number of people involved, and of their different duties. The Prefect of the Praetorian Guard, who came directly under the Emperor, was in charge of the administration of the postal service or *cursus publicus*. His inspectors, the *curiosi*, checked on the running of the posts and the strict application of the rules and regulations. In every province or district a prefect of transport (*Praefectus vehiculorum*) controlled the day-to-day organization of the service.

At the head of each station was a director (*stationarius*). He managed the slaves who carried out the work of stable boys, postillions, blacksmiths, ostlers and so on. The *stationarius* controlled the passports of the messengers and kept records of arrivals and departures.

The *tabellarii* carried the despatches along the routes; individuals could vary their actual routes, and

bendym hanaube

By the fifteenth century the German states were organizing their own messenger services, and the guild posts were declining. This foot postman (from a contemporary playing card) wears the emblem of the Duchy of Prussia.

their working hours were irregular. The postal vehicles were light, two-wheeled coaches drawn by two horses, carrying a load of about 200 kilos. Their dimensions and specifications were exactly laid down by law and were subject to careful checks. While the state had to meet the expense of the vehicles and personnel, local communities were responsible for the relay stages in their districts.

The *cursus publicus* continued to function for many centuries, until the fall of the Roman Empire and the victories of the barbarians from the north and east. Certain features of the Roman postal service lingered on, but documentary evidence from the turbulent period of the fifth to the tenth centuries is rare and imprecise. We know, however, that Theodoric, king of the Visigoths, permitted a relay system to function in Spain which dated from the time of the Romans. He gave orders that the horses used in this service should be fed and sheltered. The Breviary of Alaric enumerates the public laws in force in A.D. 506 and mentions that the use of post-horses for non-official business was forbidden.

In the eighth century, Charlemagne reigned over a vast territory covering the whole of western Europe from Denmark to the Danube and Spain. He maintained contact with his subordinates by means of messengers. These couriers, holding passports, were given priority in obtaining mounts, and any person hindering them received exemplary punishment: if he were a slave, he was stripped of clothing and his head was shaved as a mark of infamy. Under Charlemagne's weaker successors, however, the relay systems gradually disappeared as territories were again divided, and a feudal type of society developed.

THE MIDDLE AGES

During the Middle Ages, Europe witnessed the development of many different types of postal system. As it would take too much space to discuss them all here, we shall simply give examples of each type.

THE MERCHANTS' POSTS

In Germany, butchers had to make frequent journeys by carriage to buy supplies of meat from outlying farms, and for a long time they used to carry with them letters from one town to another. Eventually, the Guild of Butchers organized an actual postal administration under the name of the Butchers' Post (*Metzer Post*). Organizing the post became an important part of a butcher's job. At Essling, for example, no one could set up in business as a butcher unless he had a horse and undertook the carriage of mail as part of his duties. The arrival and departure of the butchers' couriers was announced in each town by the sound of a horn, an instrument which subsequently became the emblem of the posts, and which to this day figures in numerous badges and devices of the postal services all over the world. The *Metzer Post* survived till the reign of the Emperor Rudolph II (1576–1611), when it was absorbed into the official postal service.

In Italy, which occupied a position of paramount importance in commerce, the merchants also organized a postal service. The most important international trade fairs were held in the French county of Champagne, at Lagny, Provins, Troyes and Bar. These fairs were held six times a year. The large Italian cities (Rome, Genoa, Venice, Lucca, Bologna, Pistoia, Asti, Florence, Milan, etc.) were grouped together under the name of *Universitas Mercatorum Italiae nondinas Campaniae ac regnum Francorum frequentatium* (the University of the Italian merchants attending the fairs of Champagne and the kingdom of France). Each of these cities possessed its own couriers. In Florence the Society *Arte dei Mercanti di Calimala* had the foresight, in 1301, to add a clause to its statutes giving them the right to send two messengers to each fair. The first of these carried the orders for purchases and arrived at the beginning of the fair, while the second dealt with matters of payment and did not come until the end. The name *Calimala* came from the street in Florence where the majority of the drapers had their business and each member of the society paid a tax to the messenger. He was known as the *scarcelliere*, from the *scarcella* or saddle-bag he carried containing the letters. As Florentine bankers managed the papal fortune, this society also maintained communication with the Pope in Rome, and later in

Avignon after the Papacy moved there in 1309. There was even regular correspondence with London at the time. Private staging posts, owned by Italians, ensured the messengers an easy and safe journey.

THE UNIVERSITY POSTS

Established at the beginning of the thirteenth century, the great universities received students from all over the known world. On account of the slowness of travel in those days the students tended to stay at their university for several years, going home only at the end of their studies. In order to ensure regular communication with their families these students made use of messengers who carried letters, money and parcels. Such a system existed at Oxford, Bologna, Paris and many other medieval universities. The university of Paris, for example, was divided into four faculties (theology, law, medicine and arts) and each faculty comprised four "nations". The faculty of arts organized the messenger system. The "nation" of France in the Arts faculty sent out messengers to all corners of the country and the Mediterranean lands such as Aragon, Castile, Portugal, Italy, Corsica, Sicily, Sardinia, the Duchy of Spoleto and so forth. The "nation" of Normandy corresponded with Normandy while the "nation" of Picardy dealt with the Flemish countries. The "nation" of England sent messengers to London, Oxford, Dublin, Aberdeen, Glasgow, Bergen, Uppsala, Cracow, Hungary, Livonia, Bohemia, Gothland, Moravia, Pomerania, Silesia and throughout Germany.

All of these messengers carried letters not only for the students but also for private individuals. The profit derived from the carriage of mail was considerable and enabled the university to pay its professors! This practice survived despite attempts by the state to curtail it; in fact it was not suppressed until the development of the state postal service at the beginning of the eighteenth century. Thus the university postal service operated for five centuries, providing a regular link between all the peoples of Europe.

THE MONASTIC POSTS

The twelfth and thirteenth centuries were a period of great religious activity and some of the greatest abbeys in Europe were founded at this time. When St. Bernard died, in 1153, he had founded 35 monasteries in France, 11 in Spain, ten in England and Ireland, six in Flanders, four in Italy, two each in Germany and Sweden, one in Hungary and one in Denmark. In the same period the Cistercians possessed more than 500 monasteries in various countries.

Messengers operated a regular service between these religious houses, carrying news and instructions. The messenger was known as a *rotuliger* or a *rotularius*, from the roll of parchment (*rotulum*) the monks used for writing their letters. The message was written by the sender and carried to the next monastery, where the reader of the message would have all the monks assembled before him. A reply, which also served as an acknowledgement of receipt, would then be written by a monk, skilled in the art of calligraphy, on another leaf of parchment. This was sewn on to the bottom of the previous message and the messenger would then go off to another monastery where the process was repeated. These joined-up sheets of parchment formed a volume which was rolled around an ornamental wooden cylinder and placed inside a container. The circulation of such a roll of correspondence might take many months, if not years. The Roll of St. Vital in 1132 consisted of 206 replies on 206 stages. It went back and forward between France and England on many occasions and measures more than 9 metres long. The roll which announced the death of the Abbess Matilda, daughter of William the Conqueror, in 1113 was over 20 metres long and had been to 252 religious houses. Another roll, originated by the Abbey of Solignac, comprised 323 replies! Many of these were written on both sides of the sheet, some in prose and others in verse. This procedure continued until the fifteenth century, when the development of more modern methods of communication provided more rapid transmission of messages.

THE POSTS IN THE TOWNS

All important towns and cities maintained municipal messengers. They were responsible for carrying the letters of magistrates and civic dignitaries. There were also groups of messengers whom the ordinary public could make use of. These groups were highly organized, and were governed by statutes and regulations designed to maintain the confidence of the users.

So that these messengers could be easily recognized they wore a special livery in the colours of their city and a rather cumbersome insignia, elaborately decorated and known as a "messenger-box" (in German *Bottenbüchse*, in French *Boîte de Messager*, in Dutch *Bodebus*). Armed with a pike and sometimes accompanied by guard-dogs, they worked in all

Universities organized their own postal service in the middle ages. Jean Lequeux, Messenger of Guise en Thiérache, Diocese of Laon, is typical of messengers of this time.

A typical Benedictine rotula, dated 1501. The complete parchment, written in many different handwriting styles, measures over 5 metres.

weathers on foot or on horseback. Among the many cities with a distinctive municipal postal service were Hamburg, Tournai, Aix la Chapelle, Strasbourg, Toulouse, Basel, Marseilles, Lyons, Gouda, Amsterdam, Nijmegen, Frankfurt and Zurich.

Strasbourg is credited with being one of the earliest cities to have sworn messengers, for the archives of the former republic of Strasbourg mention *Läufferbotten* as early as 1322. The messengers were made to swear that they would be of good behaviour, pious, faithful and honest. They were not allowed to indulge in gambling, to sell their insignia for money, or to entrust letters to unauthorized persons. Tariffs varied according to the distance travelled and the weather conditions. They elected their treasurer themselves and were allowed eight ells of cloth each year for their uniform.

The study of the organization of these messengers, and of their journeys, has occupied many historians. To get some idea of the distances they had to travel it is useful to consult the post-book (*Postkursbuch*) of Sebastien Brant, Chancellor of Strasbourg from 1503 till 1521, and at the same time Director of the messenger service. This valuable work details 33 itineraries used by the messengers. If you look at a map of Europe you will get some idea of the hardships these

messengers – or indeed any traveller – had to suffer at this time. Included in the routes undertaken by these messengers were: Strasbourg to Vienna via Salzburg; Strasbourg to Vienna via Regensburg; Strasbourg to Vienna via the Arlberg and the Brenner passes; Strasbourg to Venice; Strasbourg to Rome, Lübeck, Königsberg and Memel; to Nuremberg; to Cracow via Breslau; to Prague via Pilsen; to Bamberg; to Coburg; to Milan via the St. Gotthard pass; to Glarus; to Lucerne; to Bruges via Namur; to Calais via Brussels; to Antwerp; to Lyons; to Paris, and to Le Havre. The total would run to many thousands of miles. When you realize that this was only one of the many networks existing at the time, you will appreciate the scope of the civic messenger systems. However, just as the university messenger systems disappeared when the state postal services developed, the civic posts also declined, though they lingered on and co-existed with state posts for hundreds of years.

THE MESSENGERS OF KINGS AND PRINCES

Every king and potentate maintained his own personal service of horsemen, always ready to start out with orders to the frontiers, or instructions to ambassadors, no matter how far distant. In the sixteenth century the kings of France had 120 couriers in per-

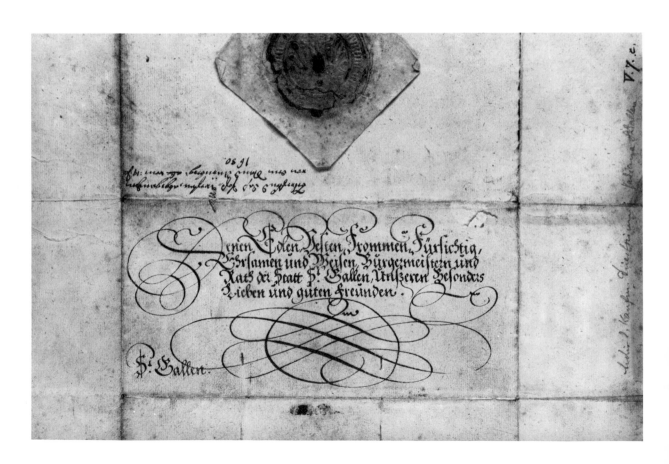

Left: In the seventeenth century most towns in Europe used municipal messengers to carry official documents. This letter, written in 1680, was sent by the Mayor of Nuremburg to the Mayor of St. Gallen.

Official city messengers carried messenger boxes, decorated with their city's emblems. This reconstruction of a sixteenth-century box comes from Berne.

manent readiness. Charles the Bold and Philip the Fair, Dukes of Burgundy, could muster dozens of horse-messengers. The Plantagenet monarchs in England also maintained special messengers to keep in constant touch with their dominions in Gascony and the Venetian Senate operated a regular service of letter-carriers to Constantinople where the Serene Republic had important economic and commercial interests. By the seventeenth century these couriers had become government messengers. Bearers of special passes, placed under the protection of their masters, they enjoyed absolute priority and by virtue of international agreements they were accorded a free passage with all the privileges which we would nowadays associate with the "diplomatic bag".

THE OFFICE OF THURN AND TAXIS

The end of the Middle Ages witnessed the rise of the family of Thurn and Taxis, a family which eventually obtained a monopoly of postal services in the greater part of Europe, and made their immense

fortune from the mail. Their monopoly survived as late as 1867. They are supposed to have taken their name from an ancestor who heroically defended a post situated in a tower during a siege of Milan at the time when St. Ambrose was the bishop there (A.D. 374). The name *della Torre* (of the tower) was rendered in French as *de Tour* and in German as *von Thurn*. Much later one of his descendants named Tacius joined the two titles, which thus became *de Tour et Tassis* or *von Thurn und Taxis*.

Every member of the Thurn and Taxis family became concerned in some way with postal matters. Count Roger I of Thurn and Taxis is known to have organized a service of post-horses between the Tyrol and northern Italy – the Emperor Frederick III knighted him in 1450 as a reward. In 1501 the Archduke of Austria, Philip I, appointed Francis of Thurn and Taxis "Captain and Master of our Posts". On January 18, 1505, Philip, now king of Castile (Spain), signed at Brussels a treaty with the same Francis, establishing a courier service between the Low Countries and the courts of Germany, Spain and France.

Left: A French royal messenger, from an illuminated manuscript of the late fifteenth century. Kings and princes maintained a corps of messengers for carrying government documents and royal letters. Protected by special international agreements, the messengers enjoyed many of the privileges diplomats are entitled to today.

Above, right: The sign of a Thurn and Taxis post house in Germany. By the eighteenth century, Thurn and Taxis offices and employees were found all over Europe.

Right: The title page of the Tassis family records, printed in Antwerp in 1645 and now on display in the Musée Postal, Brussels. As the "Taxis" half of the Thurn and Taxis family, the Tassis family played a major part in the development of the European postal service.

The following year a route linking Malines in Belgium with Innsbruck in Austria was organized.

In 1516, as a further extension, the German emperor, Maximilian I, instructed Thurn and Taxis to set up a postal link between Vienna and Brussels, and confirmed their privilege of monopoly. Charles V, ruler of an immense territory embracing Germany, Spain, Italy and the Netherlands, named Leonard of Thurn and Taxis *Oberpostmeister des Deutschen Kaiserthums* (Chief Postmaster of the German Empire). The Thurn and Taxis organization was now becoming very international and the king of France authorized the couriers of the Thurn and Taxis service to cross his territory, from Belgium to Spain via Bordeaux and from Spain to Italy via Narbonne. Staging posts were established everywhere; on the route from Brussels to Augsburg, for example, the horses were changed at 27 different places. However, each time that war broke out, or international relations were bad, the couriers were arrested and robbed of their mail.

In 1574 the postal service was placed at the disposal of the general public and no longer reserved for the use of the sovereign or his court. In that year the title of "Grand Master of the Posts" was declared to be hereditary and it was conferred on Prince Lamoral of Thurn and Taxis (1557–1624). Throughout the seventeenth century the enterprise of Thurn and Taxis expanded, and although they gradually had to face opposition from such states as the Palatinate, Brandenburg and Saxony, which preferred to organize their own postal services, there was scarcely a town of any importance that did not have an office and a postmaster. Lamoral was succeeded in office by Claudius of Thurn and Taxis (1621–76), Eugene-Alexander (1652–1714), Anselm-Francis (1681–1739), Alexander-Ferdinand (1704–73), Charles-Anselm (1733–1805), Charles-Alexander (1770–1827) and Maximilian-Charles (1802–71).

It has been estimated that by the eighteenth century the Thurn and Taxis family earned about 20,000 livres every day, and produced an annual profit of 4,000,000 livres. They employed a staff of 20,000 and possessed tens of thousands of horses and many castles and estates. (At Frankfurt am Main the palace housing the Diet of the German Confederation belonged to them.) Their postillions were instantly recognizable all over Europe by the yellow trumpet embroidered on the front and back of their tunics. They sounded a posthorn and carried a special passport.

Powerful though the Thurn and Taxis family was, their monopoly could not last forever. The Emperor Napoleon I was not well disposed towards them and when he came to power, he allowed the new states of the Confederation of the Rhine to develop their own postal systems. Despite all their diplomatic skill the Grand Masters of the Posts were unable to shore up their crumbling empire. After the defeat of Napoleon the Thurn and Taxis family managed to recover something of their former power, but before many years elapsed their postal monopoly had been reduced to three grand duchies, three duchies and a few principalities. Belgium, Württemberg, the canton of Schaffhausen in Switzerland, the Hohenzollern dominions and many of the free cities broke away from them. Nevertheless they continued to enjoy substantial revenue from their postal network and eventually, on July 1, 1867, sold their remaining rights to Prussia for 3,000,000 thalers.

The family of Thurn and Taxis had been the prime organizers of the European postal network for four centuries. Their role in the development of international relations was very great and their contribution to greater understanding between the peoples of Europe cannot be overestimated.

THE POSTS IN ASIA IN THE MIDDLE AGES

During the Middle Ages the Mongol Empire was like a magnet to the merchants of Venice and Genoa, whose caravans brought home silks, spices, porcelain and carpets from the Far East. Marco Polo, a Venetian who spent seventeen years at the court of the son of Genghis Khan, wrote an account of how the Chinese postal service functioned.

A large number of routes linked all the provinces to Peking. Along these roads 25,000 relay stations, known as *yamb*, were set up. There the messengers of the emperor were given hospitality and found excellent refreshment and fresh mounts. At each staging-post a room 'with beautiful drapes of silk'' was placed at the disposal of the messengers. All together the stables of these relay stations are estimated to have held some 200,000 horses. On the shortest routes the messengers went on foot, wearing belts hung with little bells round their waists, so that people could hear them coming.

The postal service was reserved exclusively for the transmission of official despatches and very serious penalties were meted out to private individuals who flouted this regulation. Until 1879 the Chinese government did not permit a public postal service and even in 1914 a large area was served only by a messenger system.

In Japan a similar system of relays was maintained for the sole use of the emperor. The sale of rice from the fields belonging to the postal service provided the money for the maintenance of the couriers.

THE FIRST NATIONAL POST

We have seen how, following the disappearance of the Roman postal system, courier services developed for the use of privileged sections of the community such as merchants, students and civil servants. These postal services, flourishing simultaneously, were a source of revenue for their proprietors but not for the state. During the fifteenth and sixteenth centuries, however, things began gradually to change. Bit by bit, each country began to assert its sovereignty and one of the ways they showed this was by trying to gain a monopoly on the transportation of people and mail. These states were concerned not only with questions of public order but also with political and economic problems. A strong state could not maintain itself

A surprisingly sophisticated network of posts operated in many oriental countries. This Japanese runner dates from the period before the westernization of Japan in 1868.

without some permanent control over its subjects and their activities. What easier way was there than by achieving a monopoly on the hiring out of horses? What easier way to discover the plans of suspected persons than by monopolizing the transportation of letters – and possibly opening them? What simpler method could there be of imposing a ban or a tax on certain newspapers than to be responsible for their transportation?

GERMANY

Until the end of the eighteenth century the Thurn and Taxis postal administration enjoyed a virtual monopoly of the posts in the German Empire, but by the beginning of the eighteenth century the more powerful states were struggling to organize their own postal services. Prussia was using its own distinctive postmarks by 1750. However, it was not until the establishment of the Confederation of the Rhine under the aegis of Napoleonic France in 1808 that a national postal system really began to develop. This was undone by the Treaty of Versailles which restored the old princely states, but between 1820 and 1865 most of them dispensed with the Thurn and Taxis administration and established their own systems. The movement towards postal unity was stimulated by the formation of the German-Austrian Postal Union in 1850, regulating and standardizing rates.

FRANCE

King Louis XI (1423–83) was the first ruler in the modern period to have created a horse post, mark-

A French horse postman of 1650. At that time it took 359 hours (fifteen days) for horse-relays to carry mail from Paris to Marseilles.

ing the principal routes with relay stations which his couriers used. On June 19, 1464 an edict proclaimed at Luxies (in the department of the Somme) stated:

"Relay stations with four or five horses are to be placed at intervals of four leagues (twelve miles) (article 2) . . . There is instituted a 'Grand Master of the Messengers of France' (*Grand Maître des coureurs de France*) (article 4) . . . It is forbidden to postmasters to give out horses to unauthorized persons, on pain of death (article 9) . . . All relay stations must be maintained in perfect condition (article 18) . . . Messengers are forbidden to carry the letters of the general public . . . Sworn messengers shall set out from the cities to carry the orders of the king to other towns. These horsemen will galop from one relay station to the next."

Successive kings – Charles VIII (1483–98), Louis XII (1498–1515), Francis I (1515–47), and Henry II (1547–59) – improved this institution. Henry IV and Louis XIII virtually placed the postal system at the service of the general public. In this way the service was exploited by different juridical systems according to the times, but gradually the French posts came under direct government control.

ITALY

It was in Piedmont, then part of the duchy of Savoy, that the first state postal service in Italy was established. Emmanuel-Philibert, Duke of Savoy, appointed by letters patent on January 10, 1561, a certain Messer Scaramuccia as "Postmaster-General". This postmaster-general obtained a revenue of about 700 crowns a year. Later the title became "General of the Posts and Admiral of the Po", and from the end of the sixteenth century various regulations governed the organization of the horse post. The kinship of the dukes of Savoy with the numerous ruling houses of Europe and the excellent geographical position of the country made it possible to establish important post routes between Lyons and Rome and between Lyons and Venice.

On March 10, 1604 an edict of Charles Emmanuel I gave to the state a monopoly of the carriage of letters from private individuals. In 1720 the service between

Maximilian I of Austria, surrounded by his court, gives letters and instructions to his messenger.

Right: By the early seventeenth century, foot posts existed in London and other important English cities. This Jacobean postman is reproduced from the title page of *A Straunge Foot-Post*, a pamphlet published in 1613.

A post-rider and his horn quickly became the universally accepted emblem of the post. This Italian post-rider appears on a seventeenth-century itinerary: *A new itinerary for Ottavio Codogno's post throughout the world.*

Piedmont and Geneva was established. In the same year Piedmont had 42 post offices including agencies in Nice, Alexandria, Novara and Tortone. In 1736 Piedmont won the concession of opening a postal agency in Rome and this survived until 1860. On August 12, 1818 a modern postal administration much like that in existence today was finally created.

PORTUGAL

It was in 1520 that King Emmanuel I gave to Luis Homem the appointment of Grand Master of the Posts, and this was confirmed in 1525. Homem was required to reside in Lisbon, to maintain sufficient couriers for the king's service and also for the use of the general public, and to fix the postal rates according to the distance travelled and the time taken.

The staff of this service wore the royal coat of arms on their uniform and had the right to carry a sword and a dagger. From 1532 to 1565 Luis Afonso held office, being succeeded by Francisco Coelho (1565–1577). When Coelho died, his son-in-law, Manuel de Gouveia, succeeded him. At this time there was a

A Straunge Foot-Post,

With

A Packet full of strange Petitions.

After a long Vacation for a good Terme.

Printed at London by E. A. dwelling neare Christ-Church. 1613.

weekly delivery by messenger between Lisbon and the provinces, and a monthly one to destinations in Italy and France!

The office was vacant between 1598 and 1606 and the service was run by deputies. From 1606 to 1798 the family of Mata Coronel ran the postal service with a great deal of success, in spite of drawbacks arising from their Jewish origins: anti-semitism was considerable in seventeenth-century Portugal. The palace in Lisbon, owned by the Mata family and used as the headquarters of the postal service, was destroyed in the terrible earthquake of 1755.

In 1798 Manuel José da Maternidade da Mata was indemnified by the Portuguese government, which took over the postal service and granted various pensions, honours and titles. From then onwards the Portuguese state postal service was conducted as a branch of the government service.

ENGLAND

Sovereigns such as Edward III, Elizabeth and James I had their own messengers on horseback. James I (1603–25) later organized a service to foreign parts and farmed out the monopoly. In the sixteenth century the numerous businessmen established in England, especially in London, obtained permission to set up a private postal service to the Continent known as the "Merchant Adventurers' Post". A proclamation of 1591, however, obliged all mail to be transmitted via the royal postal service. At this time there were two distinct organizations, headed respectively by Lord Stanhope, the Postmaster-General, and Matthew de Quester, whose official title was "Postmaster of England for Foreign Parts out of the King's Dominions".

In 1635 Charles I centralized the distribution of the correspondence of private individuals in England and Scotland, and separated this from the postal service employed on government business. A businessman named Billingsley tried in vain to set up a private postal service, but was sent to prison for his pains.

In 1666 the foreign service from England consisted of one messenger a week for Marseilles (ten days on the journey), two a week to Paris (a four-day journey), one a week to Madrid (26 days), Venice (15 days) and Genoa (17 days). In 1715 the kingdom was divided into six postal districts. Each district had a "riding surveyor" who was responsible for the control of the mail and the horses and for making reports to the post office in London. The British postal service quickly built up an organization which was very efficient and served as a model for those in other countries. To Britain must go the credit for having instituted many of the postal reforms.

SWITZERLAND

The confederation of thirteen cantons did not have any definite policy as far as postal matters were concerned. At St. Gallen, Zurich, Schaffhausen, Geneva, Berne and Basel there functioned local postal services which were very efficiently organized but which were quite independent of each other. In the bishopric of Basel, for example, there was a "Peasants' Post", so called because letters had to be carried free of charge by the bishop's subjects, as part of their obligations to their overlord. The bishop also had his own couriers, as had the municipalities of Delemont and Porrentruy.

The municipality of Delemont seems to have been a law to itself. In 1645 it refused a letter addressed thus: "Gentlemen Master-burgesses and Council of the Town" purely because the letter should have been addressed: "Gentlemen the Right Honourable Lords, the Master-burgesses and Council . . ."! And in 1671, in the same town, there was a woman messenger named Régine who wore with her skirt a red and white bodice (the Swiss national colours) and on her head a tricorn hat of black felt.

The Helvetic Republic decreed on September 3, 1798 that the postal service constituted a prerogative of the state, but state control was short-lived, for in 1803 the sovereignty of the cantons was re-established and each of them recommenced its own postal system. From this time the postal rates became increasingly expensive and complex. Finally the federal authorities decided to unify the service with effect from January 1, 1849, stating specifically that the revenues of the posts were to go to the federal treasury, that the secrecy of letters would be respected, and that postal rates would be reasonable. Eventually the modern Swiss postal system was established!

RUSSIA

The first Russian postal organization was founded about 1630 to meet the needs of Michael Feodorovich the first of the Romanov rulers, at a time when the great powers were beginning to send their ambassadors to Russia. The development of manufacturing industries and the influx of foreigners helped to expand the service. Peter the Great set up regular postal services between the chief towns and established post offices at Moscow in 1711 and St. Petersburg in 1717.

Alexander I, the Tsar who helped rid Europe of the menace of Napoleon, organized a network of messengers who used rapid post-coaches under the control of Prince Alexander Galitzin. The carriage of letters was relatively expensive. In the early nineteenth

The Swiss postal service remained very complicated until the middle of the nineteenth century, when the federal authorities unified the separate cantonal systems. This cover of July 1851 from La Sagna to Zurich, bears two strips of early Swiss stamps. The postal rates were levied according to the *rayon*, or radius of the post route, hence the inscription on the 10 rappen stamps. Rayon II indicated the two to ten mile radius.

century the service was regular, but the letters had to be deposited sixteen hours before the mails departed. By 1897 Russia had 9,731 post offices with a staff of 51,589 employees of all grades; the annual turnover was 220 million letters, two for every inhabitant.

UNITED STATES OF AMERICA

The American postal services may be said to have begun in 1639 when an ordinance of Massachussetts laid the foundations of a postal system with Richard Fairbanks of Boston as postmaster. In 1691 Thomas Neale was appointed to handle mail arriving from overseas and destined for the various European settlements in North America.

Two years later the Scotsman Duncan Campbell and his son John put the mail service on a proper footing. They established a newspaper called *The Boston Newsletter* which circulated in the same manner as the letters. Every fifteen days a messenger set out from Boston for New York and another departed from New York for Boston. These couriers delivered letters along the way and exchanged mailbags at Say Brook. This system was in operation by 1714.

In 1737 Philadelphia was connected with Newport (Virginia), a messenger named Henry Pratt setting out at the beginning of each month and returning 24 days later. In 1742 letters went from Philadelphia to New York every eight days in summer and every fifteen days in winter. At this time Benjamin Franklin was Postmaster of Philadelphia. In 1753 he became Postmaster-General and seven years later Albany was linked by a postal service to Boston.

After the annexation of Quebec and Florida by Britain at the end of the Seven Years War (1756–63), the postal system in British North America was divided into two districts. The northern district (from Quebec to Virginia) was entrusted to Franklin. The southern district (the Carolinas and Florida) was entrusted to Benjamin Barrows. In turn his successors were Pierre de Lancrey and George Roupell. The postal headquarters for this area were at Charleston.

After the Declaration of Independence the postal system developed rapidly. Postal routes were farmed out to concessionaires on seven-year leases and ran Boston–Albany, New York–Connecticut, Baltimore–Annapolis and Philadelphia–Pittsburgh. In 1792 the mail-coach network covered 1875 miles and there were 76 post offices.

By the early nineteenth century, when Louisiana was annexed to the United States, the postal system extended from New Orleans to Natchez and from Kahoka to St. Louis. At the same time a project for a

A Russian birch-bark letter of the twelfth century. The letter is from a magistrate, writing to Mikalu about a lawsuit involving the barter of a female slave abducted from a princess.

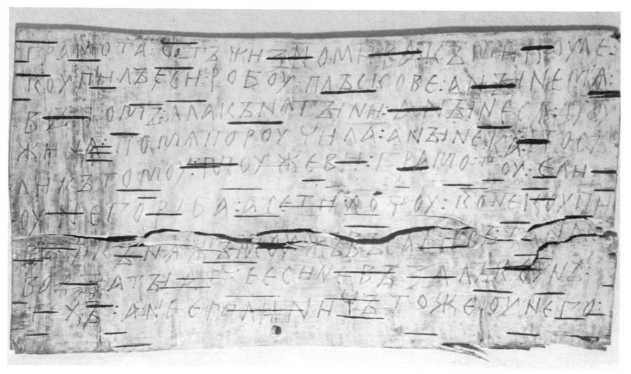

The globe encircled by letter communications — the monument to the Universal Postal Union, outside the Standehaus in Berne, Switzerland. The Standehaus has been the headquarters of the Union since its inception in 1874.

Above, left: Benjamin Franklin was Deputy Postmaster-General of the American Colonies, and first Postmaster-General of the United States. His portrait appears on one of two stamps in the first series of adhesive stamps issued in the United States.

A montage of portraits of the delegates from the fifteen countries and postal administrations represented at the Paris Postal Conference in 1863, forerunner of the Universal Postal Union.

postal link-up as far as Washington on the Pacific coast was considered. After a period in which the posts were developed by private enterprise the postal services were taken over by each state of the Union, the United States having to this day a unique postal administration, though finally under federal control.

THE UNIVERSAL POSTAL UNION

Now that the majority of the great countries were developing a national postal system, and industrial and commercial growth was taking place, the need for international postal agreements began to be felt. Each country began to negotiate for the exchange or the transmission of correspondence with its neighbours. This resulted in a multitude of treaties of the greatest complexity. In the nineteenth century, when weights gradually became standardized, Britain and the United States used the ounce, while Germany and Austria used the zolloth and France and Belgium used grammes. Units of weight were different everywhere.

A letter from Germany to Rome cost 68 pfennigs if it went via Switzerland, 90 if it crossed Switzerland and went to Genoa on a French packet-boat, 48 pfennigs via Austria and 85 via France. Each country had a bewildering number of different postage rates.

The Postmaster-General of the United States, backed up by his government, took the initiative in calling for a conference, which met in Paris from May 11 to June 8, 1863. Fifteen countries sent delegates to discuss the principal needs of international mail-handling. This conference did not manage to reach any practical conclusion but it shed light on the majority of the problems involved. Many of the bilateral agreements made after 1863 were inspired by the deliberations of the Paris Postal Conference.

On that occasion the following countries were represented: Austria, Belgium, Costa Rica, Denmark, Ecuador, Spain, France, Great Britain, Italy, the Netherlands, Portugal, Prussia, Hawaii, Switzerland, the U.S.A. and the Hanseatic cities.

Eventually the German Empire revived the concept of an international postal union and in the spring of 1873 proposed a world conference for September of the same year. The German postal minister prepared a provisional programme for discussion, but because of a request for an adjournment by Russia the conference did not take place as planned. In January 1874 Germany made a new proposition. At the invitation of the Swiss federal council, delegates from 22 countries met on September 15, 1874 at Berne. It was in the Standehaus in Berne, subsequently popularized by numerous postcards illustrating the work of the Union, that the conference took place. Among the nations represented at the 1874 conference were Egypt, Greece, Hungary, Luxembourg, Norway, Rumania, Russia, Serbia, Sweden and Turkey, as well as those which had previously met (but not Costa Rica). An agreement was reached on October 9, and was ratified at Berne on May 5, 1875. It took effect from July 1, 1875, except in France where the matter, referred to the French parliament, was delayed by six months!

British India was the first new country to apply for membership of the General Postal Union as it was then known, and a limited congress decided on the admission of the French colonies, with effect from July 1, 1876. Brazil, the Spanish colonies and Dutch overseas territories followed soon after. One of the earliest activities of the Union was the publication, in three languages, of L'Union Postale.

The second congress, held at Paris in 1878, was attended by delegates from 38 countries, seated round the same table. The name "Universal Postal Union" dates from this time. At Lisbon in 1885, 53 countries were represented, while at Vienna in 1891 and Washington in 1897 there were 56 countries. These congresses, held at regular intervals since then, have gradually embraced all the countries of the world, with the exception of Mongolia and some of the islands in the Indian Ocean. The congresses are held on democratic principles and each country, large or small, has a say in their deliberations. The sharing out of postal charges has been abolished and each country now keeps the revenue from all the letters posted within its territory, uniform tariffs being fixed as if all countries formed a single entity. Of all the old-established international institutions, the Universal Postal Union is the only one which has survived and which continues to make constant progress.

Over the years, smaller unions have been absorbed into the framework of the UPU. In 1911 the South-American Postal Union (formed for the purpose of improving the tariffs) and in 1931 the Ibero-American Postal Union were amalgamated with the UPU. The five countries of Scandinavia form a postal union of Northern Countries, offering preferential tariffs to one another. In 1935 the African Postal Union was founded while the most recent, the Arab Postal Union, was started in 1954.

At the Paris Congress held in 1947 it was decided that the UPU should constitute a specialized agency of the United Nations Organization. This connection has somewhat bedevilled procedure for discussions in the Postal Union, although it has not led it astray from its stated object: the improvement of communications between the peoples of the world.

One of the numerous caricatures of Mulready's pompous design which brought the pictorial letter sheet to an ignominious end in 1841.

2

Letters, postmarks and stamps

IN THE earliest times only the most prominent people had the right, or indeed the ability to write letters; no one else was of any consequence! After the clay tablets mentioned in the earliest histories, the Greeks wrote on the skins of animals and the Romans used wax tablets and a stylus; examples of these early letters are preserved in many museums in Europe. Thanks to the Egyptians, papyrus, a type of rush cultivated in the Nile Delta, became popular as a writing material and was eventually used as such by all the civilized countries of that period. Until the sixth century A.D. papyrus, though very expensive, was the most widely used material. Gradually, however, it was superseded by parchment, made from calfskin or the hides of goats and sheep tanned in a special way. One advantage of parchment was that, unlike papyrus, both sides could be written on. Finally, paper came from China via the Arab world to Europe. Manufactured first from cotton fibres, then from rags and wood pulp, paper rapidly ousted its rivals and remains to this day the principal material used for writing.

After the stylus came the sharpened reed, the paintbrush and then the bird's feather as a means of writing. Ancient manuals give details on how to cut and prepare feathers for use as quill pens. Indeed the very word pen is derived from the Latin word for a feather, while the French still use the word *plume*, which means both feather and pen.

Letters were sealed in the middle by narrow wrappers of parchment, the ends of which were joined together over the folds of the letter and held in place by a blob of wax impressed with a seal. Much later, about the twelfth century, letters were sealed by a wax seal applied directly across the edges of the folded letter, though this practice was slow to come into general use. The parchment wrapper was replaced by a tiny silk ribbon threaded through the letter and held in place by the wax.

There were many different ways of folding letters in order to close them easily, and a variety of methods can be seen in surviving letters of the seventeenth and eighteenth centuries. When envelopes were invented, they consisted at first of a sheet of paper cut and folded by the sender with four overlapping corners, closed with a seal. Envelopes were not manufactured commercially until the end of the eighteenth century.

POSTAL MARKINGS

The earliest letters, like those of the present day, bore on the front the address written by the sender. This address was very simple, since street numbers and, even less, postal districts, did not exist. They often consisted of no more than the name of the addressee, and the town or village. Sometimes one sees a superscription "Where he is to be found" or some similar form of wording, meaning that if the addressee were travelling, the messenger would have to catch up with him on his journey. Often the address would be quite descriptive, indicating that the addressee lived near such and such a bridge or a particular church.

When someone wanted to send a very urgent letter he would write on the front *cito* or *citissime*, the Latin for "speedily" or "very quickly". In 1613, for example, King Gustavus Adolphus of Sweden wrote to Ebba Brahe with the endorsement *Den edle wälborna Joinfru Ebba greffwe datter till Wisingsborgh Kärligen tillhande, citissime.* (To the noble miss Ebba daughter of the Count of Wissingsborgh, to be delivered lovingly, very urgent). The endorsement *cito, citissime, volantissime* which may be translated as "quick, very quickly, fly very quickly" is also to be found. Another practice was to press a small feather into the soft wax of the seal, to symbolize rapidity. In countries using the French language the words *en diligence* (with speed and care) indicated the urgency with which the letter was to be handled.

Sometimes a little cross was made on the address side of the letter, to recommend the missive to Providence. An appeal to divine protection is often found on letters entrusted to a ship's captain, when the formula might read "By this ship which God preserve". Letters despatched by mail-coach might be endorsed with the words *à la garde de Dieu* or "God guard these". Sometimes these pious inscriptions were abbreviated to the initials QDG (*qui Dieu garde*) or QDC (the Latin form *Quam Deus Conservat*).

Another endorsement which figured for a long time on the address side of letters was the price arranged between the messenger and the sender, the sum being payable by the person who received the letter. You will find, for example, *payez dix sols au porteur* (pay ten sols to the bearer) or "Pay fifteen shillings to the messenger if it arrives before Sunday". For many

A Danish postman, 1840. In many European countries in the eighteenth and nineteenth centuries, postmen collected letters by walking around the streets striking a gong or ringing a bell in order to attract business. Bellmen continued to operate in some provincial English towns as late as 1846.

Below, left: A Roman "letter" of the first century A.D., with stylus and seals. Most Roman letters were written with a reed pen and ink on papyrus. If the letter was for someone living nearby, however, it was sometimes inscribed with a stylus on wax-covered, folding wooden tablets (*codicilli*). The recipient could erase the message and use the tablets again for his reply.

An interesting example of an early express letter. The letter, from Robert Clarke to the Commissioners of the Admiralty and Navy at Whitehall, was posted on 16 July 1653 and is endorsed "Haste, Haste, Post Haste". Important government letters of this sort had to be endorsed by the postmasters en route, giving the exact times at which the letter passed through their hands. This letter bears the superscriptions of Dover (past 12 at noon, 19 July) and Sittingbourne (20 July, six at night).

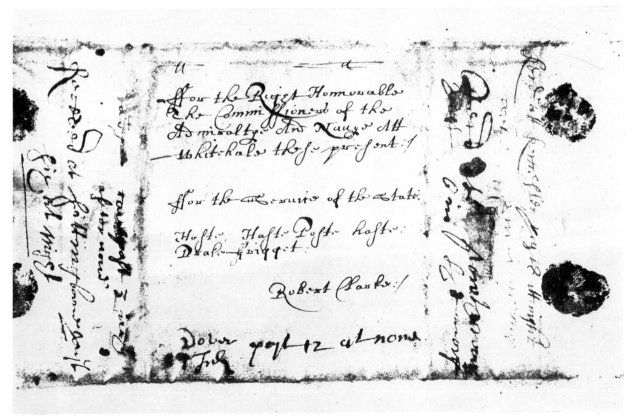

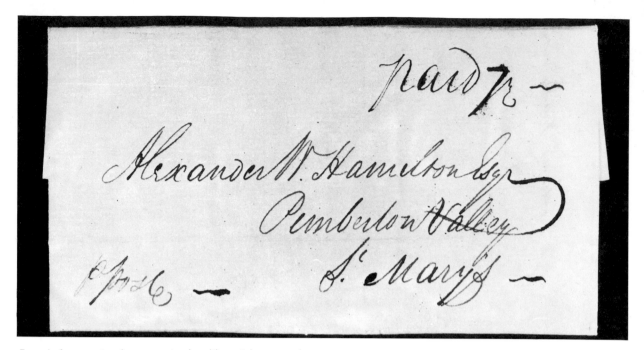

Even before postmarks were struck with metal or wooden stamps they were indicated in manuscript, and this practice survived in some parts of the world up to the introduction of adhesive stamps in the mid-nineteenth century. This early nineteenth-century example from Jamaica is endorsed "Pd 7½" indicating that the postage of 7½ pence had been prepaid.

A letter despatched to Batavia in 1791, by the East India Company ship *IJstroom*. It bears the letters D G G (*Dien God Geleide*, May God guide her), and has 2 VOC postage-due marks to the value of 6 stuivers.

centuries it was customary to make payment to the messenger when he delivered the letter, and this habit prevailed during the greater part of the period when the posts were uncertain and there was little guarantee that a letter would arrive safely at its destination. It was not until the middle of the nineteenth century that the custom disappeared.

Finally, there are the markings applied by the postal service. These were intended primarily to calculate the postage due from the recipient and gave details of the place of posting, the weight of the letter and the price to be paid.

PLACE OF POSTING

The postmaster, or official who took the letter from the sender, marked on the address side the name of the place of posting. This was in manuscript and might be given in full, or, more often, in an abbreviated form. Gradually, in order to speed up the process, name-stamps, with the place-name engraved on metal or hardwood, replaced these cumbersome manuscript endorsements. As a rule the name was given in one line, such as DE GENEVE which is found on letters from Geneva in 1695; or an abbreviation might be given in an ornamental frame. The letters P.T. IN. R., the letters signifying *Posta Toscana in Roma* (the

Tuscan post in Rome) are found within a heart-shaped device. The oldest example of such a name-stamp is of this type and was used at Milan in 1459. One other example of an early postmark has been recorded, on a letter addressed to Leonardo da Vinci in 1519. This letter was posted at Aleppo and bears the two words POSTA CECA on the seal. This curious formula has puzzled scholars who have given free rein to their imaginations but have not yet been able to find a solution or a positive meaning for this cachet!

An important name in the history of postmarks is that of Colonel Henry Bishop. A veteran of the Civil War, who served under Charles I of England, he was once saved by his little dog. After a military defeat he was being chased by a Roundhead patrol and hid himself in a closet in which the animal lay sleeping. When the soldiers came the little dog pretended to be asleep, so that the troopers would think that his master had run away! Later he was appointed by Cromwell (whose troops had once hunted him down) as Postmaster-General and he was allowed to keep his title on the accession of King Charles II. On August 2, 1661 Bishop published an ordinance announcing the introduction of a "stamp" which was to be struck on all letters. This mark bore the date on which the letter

Colonel Sir Henry Bishop, Postmaster-General of England 1660–63, introduced a postal mark showing the date on which a letter was received by the post office.

Right: Letters which were undelivered for some reason were sent to the Returned Letter Office in London, for onward transmission to the sender. These returned letters were enclosed in a wrapper: in this example of 1828 the inside of the wrapper gives interesting details concerning the operation of the London Twopenny Post. Note the hand-struck "2" to denote the postage due from the sender.

An early type of the famous Bishop mark, on a letter from London of 28 April 1673. This simple but effective date-stamp, the first of its kind used anywhere in the world, was adopted in London in 1661.

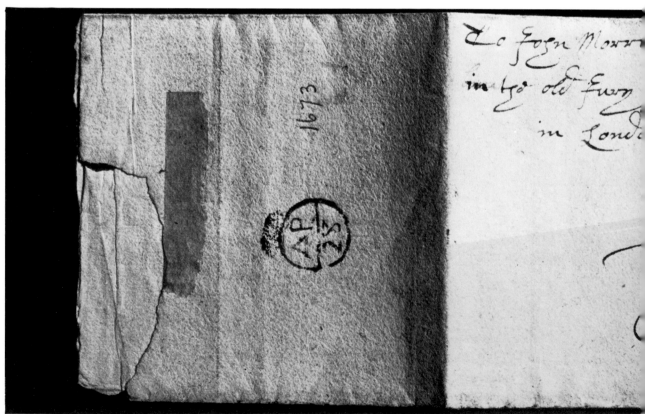

was received by the post office. It was first used in London but was gradually extended to other important cities in the kingdom. The Bishop Mark is believed to be the first postal marking to contain date plugs.

Since then there have been many thousands of postmarks in every country of the world and nowadays the collecting of postmarks is attracting numerous devotees. The marks take many different forms. In 1849 the town of Christiania (Oslo), for example, used a mark in the form of a rectangle with cut sides inscribed CHRISTIANIA 1849 9/2 (indicating the day and the month), while in 1820 a postmark used at St. Clairville, Ohio had the letters punched in a circle, with the month (June) in the centre and the day (24) inserted in manuscript by the postmaster.

Certain postmarks are ornamented by a crown, an eagle, a fleur-de-lys, a lion, or some fishes. Others have geometric figures such as stars, triangles and circles enclosing the numerals and lettering.

THE WEIGHT

The weight of a letter is rarely found inscribed in postmarks, but there is a manuscript example dating from the eighteenth century: $\frac{1}{2}$ *once faible* (half ounce deficient). Much later, when many countries adopted the metric system, postal markings bearing weights expressed in grammes were adopted, usually to denote underpaid items on which a fee had to be paid.

THE POSTAL RATE

Marks bearing a figure referring to the cost of the letter are more common. Such marks are usually known as currency marks and were applied to mail going from one country to another to indicate the correct amount of postage to be recovered from the addressee.

To these various types of marking other indications were gradually added as the techniques of the postal services developed. These include marks indicating transit, arrival, the type of letter or postal packet, instructions for return to the sender or giving reasons for the delay or non-delivery of the item. These marks exist in many different languages and their infinite variations still provide the postal historian with a vast amount of material for research and study.

THE POSTAGE STAMP

It is hard to imagine the complexity of a postal official's work 150 or 200 years ago. The charging of letters gave rise to a whole system of accountancy.

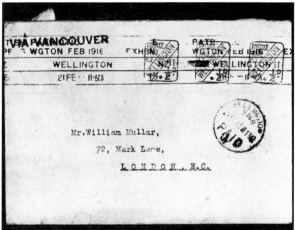

Postal markings continued to grow more complicated right up to the twentieth century. This cover, sent from New Zealand to England in February 1916, bears three strikes of New Zealand $\frac{1}{2}$d metre marks. New Zealand was the first country in the world to use metre marks. The cover also bears the Wellington Foreign Mails branch paid hand stamp, and the Wellington slogan postmark advertising the British Patriotic exhibition, Wellington, 1916. This, the second slogan postmark ever used in New Zealand, appeared more than a year before Britain adopted slogan cancellations.

Edele Agtbaare Heeren

D: Heeren Directeuren
Van den Levand sen handel
& Navigatie ind' middelantse
Zeez zer zer zer
Residerende
tot
Amsterdam

A letter despatched at the beginning of the French Revolution, 1790, still using the pre-revolutionary form of address, *Monsieur*.

Left: A letter dated 22 September, 1714, from Rotterdam to Amsterdam, with an Amsterdam postage-due mark to the value of 3 S (Stuivers), bearing the letter R (Rotterdam). These Amsterdam postage-due marks are among the oldest in the world.

The interior of a French sorting office in the reign of King Louis XV (mid-eighteenth century). Note the leather satchels used by French postmen down to the present day, and the postmarks, differing little in shape from those still in use.

Each postmaster received a bundle of letters accompanied by a way-bill setting out the cost of their carriage, which had to be recovered from each addressee and sent in to the central administration. Similarly, the messenger or postman would be responsible for handing in the cash on his return. If by chance the sender wished to pay the postage in advance he had to go to the post office, which might be a long way off, and pay over a sum of money which varied considerably according to the weight of the letter and the distance it had to be carried. One expected a letter carried 600 miles to be much dearer than a similar one carried only 60 miles; consequently the range of tariffs was vast. In France, the system of the postage paid in advance being placed in a circular envelope in a little bag attached to the letter operated until December 31, 1783. The postmaster at the receiving end collected the money due on this letter in the same way as for an ordinary letter. One cannot help thinking that the highwaymen of that period had some ripe pickings!

Several attempts were made to sell to the public sheets of paper which were already stamped, in order to cut out many of the clumsy formalities in the calculation of postage.

There is, for example, an ordinance of the Venetian Republic dated November 12, 1608 publicizing the sale of stamped sheets at a cost of 4 sols each. These sheets are inscribed with the Lion of St. Mark, with the letters A and Q on each side of it. While the sheets were carried free of postage it should be noted that the stamp indicated a fiscal, rather than a postal, tax.

The first prepaid letter sheets in the true sense were those sold in France in 1653. *Billets de port payé* (literally "tickets of prepaid postage") were invented by Jean-Jacques Renouard de Villayer, a Counsellor of State under Louis XIV and a Breton nobleman with an inventive turn of mind. Among his inventions was a watch for use at night. "He has placed within reach, near his bedside, a clock with a stout dial on which the figures of the hours had a little hollow filled with different spices. Thus to tell the time in the darkness, one needed only to follow the hand of the clock to the appropriate hollow, dip the finger in the spice and by tasting it know immediately what hour of the night it was." He had also invented an apparatus which was successfully installed on behalf of the Dauphin at Paris, Chantilly and Versailles and was described as "a flying chair which, by means of counterweights, rises and descends between two walls to whichever floor you wish." This device in fact anticipated the lifts and elevators of the present day! Unfortunately it broke down one day between two floors as it was carrying the daughter-in-law of Philip of Orleans. It took workmen three hours to rescue the hapless princess through a hole in the wall. Nothing more was ever heard of the "flying-chairs".

The third invention of Villayer is the one which is of greatest interest to postal historians. To facilitate the exchange of correspondence in Paris he erected mailboxes at the principal intersections of the streets. The boxes were emptied by postmen three times a day, and the letters taken to a central point to be redirected to every part of the city. All you had to do was buy a *billet de port payé* for one sou, date it, and fix it to the letter. The stamped wrapper was removed by the postal official and the letter then carried to the addressee. Villayer also anticipated the style of pre-paid postal stationery we use today in such different circumstances.

Unfortunately the mailboxes did not prove successful and they quickly went out of use. Practical jokers kept dropping filth and garbage into the boxes so that the letters were soiled, and mice had a nasty habit of chewing them up. No examples of the *billets* have so far come to light, although their existence is well documented in contemporary accounts and ballads.

On November 17, 1818 the postal administration of Sardinia announced the release of stamped postal paper (*Carta postale bollata*), which was to be sold in all post offices. The use of this paper was compulsory for any person sending a letter "by foot-messenger or in any other way". Each sheet bore a cachet with a galloping horse ridden by a little messenger sounding a posthorn. The format of this device was round for 15 centesimi (on a letter going up to 15 miles), oval for the 25 centesimi (on letters going from 15 to 35 miles)

Below, right: The embossed letter sheet introduced in Sydney, New South Wales in 1838. The embossed seal of the colony signified the prepayment of penny postage on letters within the city limits of Sydney. These sheets anticipated the Mulready envelopes of Britain by two years.

Two examples of *cavallini* (little horsemen), showing the circular (15 centesimi) and (above) oval (25 centesimi) types.

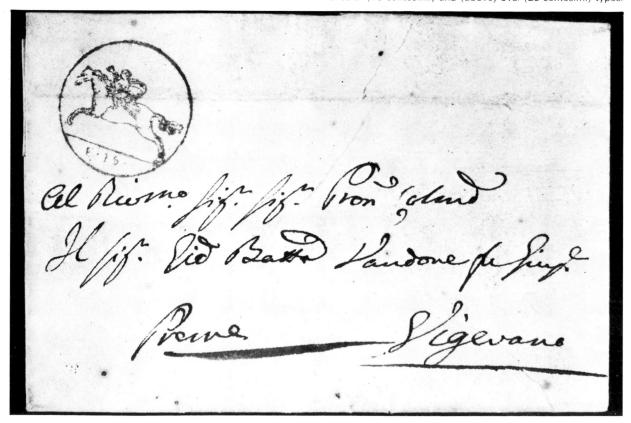

and octagonal for the 50 centesimi (for letters going beyond 35 miles). In 1820 the stamps were printed on watermarked paper. This system lasted until 1836. These marks are popularly known as the *cavallini* or *cavalotti* (little horsemen). They circulated on correspondence all over the kingdom of Sardinia including Savoy and the county of Nice. As the charge raised on these sheets was a tax designed to exercise government control on correspondence, they cannot be regarded as postage stamps in the true sense, though of course such sheets were often exempt from further payments of postage.

The idea of having some kind of official postage seems to have been widespread around this time. In 1823 in Sweden, Lieutenant Curry Gabriel von Treffenberg proposed to the government a system of prepaid sheets which could be used as letter wrappers, but this idea was not implemented. About the same time there was a system in China whereby the various classes of official mail were indicated by "stamps" in various colours. The value of these stamps was expressed in local currency. In 1838 the government of the Australian colony of New South Wales introduced letter sheets and wrappers in Sydney, the postage being indicated by means of the colonial seal embossed in colourless relief. These stamped letter sheets did not prove popular with the citizens of Sydney and though they remained in use until 1850, fine used examples are now very hard to find.

Everywhere men were trying to find some mechanical method of simplifying the mails but until 1840 when the adhesive postage stamp came into being, no one reached a satisfactory solution.

THE BIRTH OF ADHESIVE STAMPS

In 1834 there lived in Dundee in Scotland a certain James Chalmers, director and publisher of the weekly *Dundee Chronicle*. Along with the London publisher, Charles Knight, he agitated for the adoption of wrappers to prepay the postage on newspapers. Chalmers suggested a piece of paper cut out in a circle and resembling a seal, which would enable the sender to prepay the postage. He produced samples at his printing works but these never got further than the bottom of a drawer in his desk. We shall return to these specimens later.

In 1836 an accountant in Vienna proposed to the Austrian government a plan for the prepayment of postage by means of a stamp. Laurenc Koschier or Kosir, was born in Ljubljana (Laibach) and spent a lifetime in the Austrian government service. He was unable to interest the authorities in his proposals,

though many years later he was claimed by Austria and Yugoslavia as the "ideological creator of the postage stamp".

In June 1952 a special commission was convened at Millstatt in Carinthia (Austria), barely six miles from Klagenfurt and not far from the Yugoslav frontier. Composed of experts of various kinds, the commission met to examine a letter dating from early 1839. Written by a Frau Egarter to her daughter Konstanzia, this letter had lain inside the cover of a missal with a bundle of family papers. The letter was recovered shortly before the Second World War by the owner of the book, Frau Gmeiner, the wife of an Austrian engineer, but she forgot all about it again until the end of the war. This letter, whose authenticity has been attested, was sent from Spittal and addressed to Klagenfurt, and bore in addition to the normal postmarks (the date and the inscription FRANCO) a brown label bearing the numeral 1. The label was cancelled with pen strokes. Konstanzia

Egarter's father was the postmaster of Spittal, and it seems that, probably inspired by Koschier's proposals, he established a system using stamps to certify that he had received the price of the postage. This practice, however, was of very short duration and it seems likely that it was very rarely applied. Indeed, it is a miracle that this letter has come down to us intact. This first adhesive postage stamp has been declared a national treasure and is reported to have made a small fortune for its owners.

The history of the second stamp in the world (considered prior to 1952 as the first) also has picturesque elements. In 1836 a schoolmaster's son named Rowland Hill spent a holiday at a village in the north of Scotland. Born at Kidderminster in 1795 he was 37 years old when he produced a pamphlet urging improvements in the social condition of the underprivileged. He was a member of a society for popular education and had a philanthropic turn of mind.

It is said, though this may be apocryphal, that by

Right: An entire letter from Canada to England in 1847–48, the postmarks indicating the route and the time taken. It started at Hornby on December 23, 1847 and went via Palermo (January 13, 1848) to Montreal (January 18) and Toronto (date indecipherable). It reached Lancaster on February 12 and was stamped on arrival at Kirkby Lonsdale the following day. Note the dates inserted in manuscript on the Hornby and Palermo postmarks, the rate mark (1 shilling 2 pence) in manuscript and the endorsement "Too Late" indicating that the letter missed a connection at some point.

A merchant's letter from Constantinople, January 1845. Note the bilingual address, and the seal-type postmark of the Turkish post office.

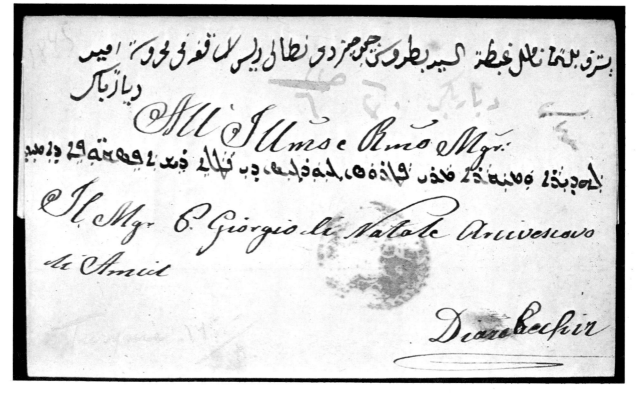

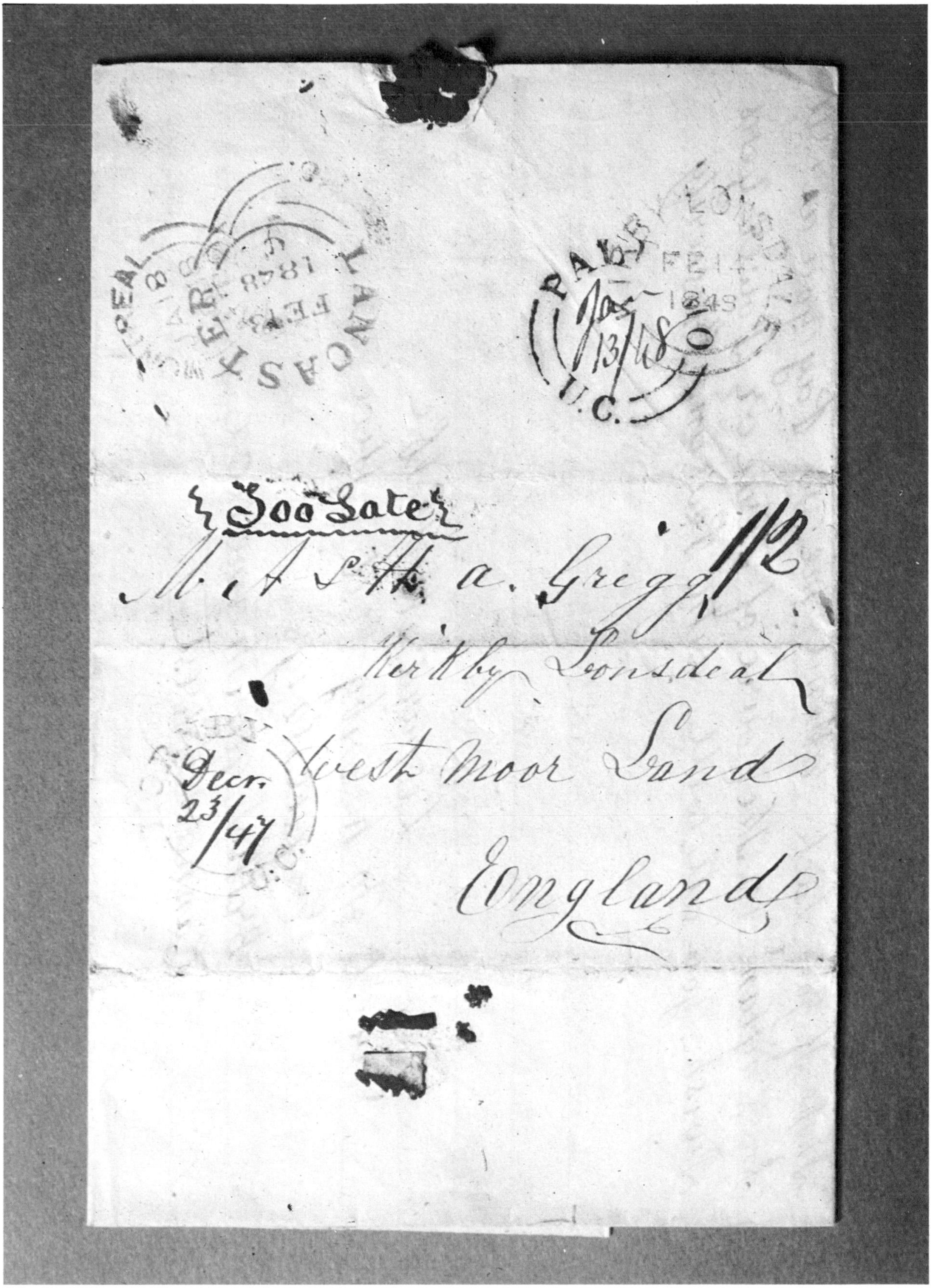

Postmarks: WESTMORLAND MAR 8 1848 / LANCASTER FEB 1848 / PARRY LONDSDALE FEB 1848 / Jas 13/48 U.C.

Too Late

M. A. S. M. a. Gregg 1/2

Kerkby Lonsdeal

West Moor Land

England

Decr 23/47

Sir Rowland Hill (1795–1879), the great postal reformer who introduced Uniform Penny Postage in 1840.

chance he witnessed a touching scene. A postman brought a letter from London addressed to a young village girl. She examined the letter but because the postage on it was very great she refused to accept it. Rowland Hill intervened but the girl was clearly embarrassed by his action. Patiently he questioned her and she finally confessed that the letter was from her fiancé working in London, but as she was too poor to afford letters from him, they had devised a neat stratagem. By means of various simple signs and marks drawn on the covering of the letter, the young man was able to let her know that he was keeping well and that he still loved her. Rowland Hill was profoundly disturbed by this story and he pondered on the problem. He concluded that there was a vicious circle in which high postal charges caused a diminution in the number of letters carried and this, in turn, forced the rates up in order to make the postal services pay their way. One way of breaking the circle would be to introduce prepayment of postage and thus eliminate the current cumbersome methods of accounting for postage. From this he deduced that a uniform rate of postage would make accountancy even simpler.

He published a pamphlet entitled *Postal Reform: its importance and the means of realizing it* in which he

The pictorial wrapper designed by William Mulready, RA, with its vignettes symbolizing the communication of Britannia with the far-flung British Empire. Parodies of this design were immensely popular and hastened the withdrawal of the Mulready wrappers from use.

W. MULREADY. R.A.   POSTAGE ONE PENNY.   JOHN THOMPSON

explained his proposals and added a note on the practical advantages, envisaging the enormous social progress which even the humblest classes would enjoy as a result. He proposed "small stamped labels" which could be sold in advance and attached to the letter by the sender. As a result a committee was formed and more than four million signatures were collected in favour of the project. Hill, helped by James Chalmers, strove by every available means, including the press, to influence public opinion. Parliament could not ignore the movement – though not all the members approved of it. The Postmaster-General, the Earl of Lichfield, opposed reform on the grounds that in order to balance his budget it would be necessary to increase the volume of mail twelvefold. Hill replied that the post offices had been tailored to the amount of mail they handled – and not the other way round. The Earl of Lichfield thought that the plan proposed "contained the most extraordinary of all the foolish and visionary ideas which he had ever read and which he would not waste breath on discussing". Colonel Maberley, Secretary to the Post Office, also considered the scheme to be unworkable.

However, on September 16, 1839 Hill was given a temporary appointment at the Treasury in order to supervise the introduction of his reforms. Despite the hostility of the postal authorities, he managed to get the support of the progressive elements in Parliament. A letter sent to Hill at this period by his brother states: "That a stranger should be bold enough to attempt to penetrate the mysteries of our postal service was something which those who had the professional charge found disagreeable; but that he should be so successful was even worse!"

Hill's effect was tremendous: he undoubtedly had a knack for publicity. His supporting committee, which consisted of 12 London businessmen, published a little periodical, *The Post Circular*, which was distributed free of charge. It also published numerous petitions and gathered thousands of signatures. One of the pamphlets it issued was entitled *Examples of Postal Charges in 1839, to be preserved as Curiosities in Museums*. A poster proclaimed "Mothers and fathers who wish to have news of your absent children; Friends who are separated and wish to write to each other; Emigrants who do not want to forget your mother land; Farmers who want to know the best places to sell your produce; Workers and labourers who want to know or find the best work and the highest wages; Support the report of the House of Commons by your petitions in favour of the Uniform Penny Post . . . That each city, town or village, each corporation, each society or religious congregation . . . should sign . . . a petition. This is not a party-political question."

The merchant classes were in favour of the reforms, as were the majority of the people, and eventually a parliamentary commission was established, drew up a proposal and the Prime Minister, Lord Melbourne, put it to the vote. The vote went in favour of Hill's proposal, in both the House of Commons and in the House of Lords. The text adopted on December 26, 1839 outlined four methods of prepaying postage: the purchase of stamped letter sheets, the impression of a stamp on paper of one's own choice, the purchase of stamped envelopes, and the purchase of adhesive stamps which could be attached to the letter. In December 1839 a Uniform Fourpenny Post was introduced, as a prelude to the Penny Post which was established on January 10, 1840. This massive cut in postal charges produced enormous bottle-necks of mail handled at the post office counters. On the first day alone some 112,000 letters were posted in London.

A great competition was held in which the public were invited to submit patterns for the proposed postage stamps and envelopes. More than 2,500 entries were examined by the judges. The winning envelope was designed by the painter William Mulready and engraved by John Thomson. It is worth a detailed description. In the middle was the figure of Britannia with a British lion at her feet. She was surrounded by winged messengers, whom she despatched in all directions. On the right hand side were a group of Quakers reading a letter and some Indian chiefs with their squaws and young children. On the same side a group of negroes manhandled casks under the direction of a white overseer, and nearby was a European woman reading a letter to her children. In the centre, behind Britannia was a reindeer drawing a sledge while, to the left, was a fleet of sailing ships. The Orient was symbolized by camels and elephants in the upper left-hand corner, and below them were Indian scribes in a bazaar. In the lower left-hand corner was a couple reading a letter from an absent friend. What remained of the space in the middle was intended for the address. The design was not at all successful and was, in fact, ridiculed by the general public. It inspired numerous caricatures and parodies, in many of which Britannia was replaced by a blowsy old hag sailing in a tub. The Mulready envelopes and wrappers were hastily withdrawn from use and the remaining stock was subsequently incinerated in a furnace constructed for this purpose!

By contrast, however, adhesive stamps were an enormous success, far beyond the calculations of the printers, Perkins, Bacon and Petch. They worked non-stop, producing 500,000 stamps a day, in order to have a sufficient quantity ready by May 6, 1840, the first day of issue. There were two stamps, known,

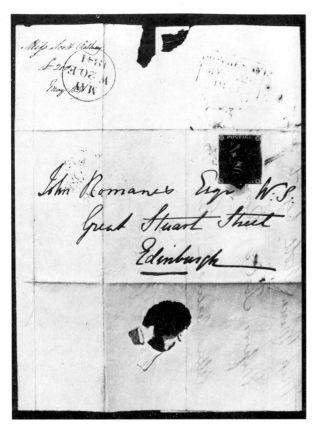

on account of their colours, as the Penny Black and the Twopence Blue. They bore the effigy of the young Queen Victoria, her crowned head facing left. It stands out against a finely chequered background, bordered with delicately engraved spandrels intended to defeat the would-be forger. Across the top was the word POSTAGE and across the foot the value expressed in words. In the upper corners was a star device, while different combinations of letters appeared in the two lower corners.

The penny stamp prepaid postage to any part of the kingdom, on a letter weighing up to half an ounce. Before Hill's reforms the same letter would have cost eightpence for a distance up to 80 miles alone and more for a longer journey. Not surprisingly, the number of letters carried rose very rapidly.

A public subscription was raised on behalf of Rowland Hill. The highest sum received was ten guineas and the final total amounted to over £15,725. Parliament voted a gratuity of £20,000 to Hill and he was later made a Knight Commander of the Bath. He died in Hampstead at the age of 84. His statue outside the General Post Office in London is inscribed simply "He created a Uniform Penny Postage, 1840". The postage stamp was born, and was destined to have a great future throughout the world.

The Penny Black, the world's first adhesive stamp, on a letter from Rothesay, Isle of Bute in 1840. The design was engraved from a medal by William Wyon. The colour of the stamp used was changed to red in 1841, so that the postmark could be seen more easily.

Below: Envelope from Dublin to Monaghan, Ireland, June 1856. The Penny Red stamp bears an experimental "duplex" postmark used in Dublin for a short period. It combines the office number "186" with the diamond-shaped date-stamp.

One of the most valuable covers in existence, this envelope from Hawaii in October 1852 bears examples of the 2 and 5 cents stamps first issued in Hawaii in 1851, together with a pair of the contemporary American 3 cent stamps. The early stamps of Hawaii, type-set in Honolulu, are known to collectors as "missionaries", from the fact that most of the known examples were on mail sent by American missionaries in Hawaii to friends and relatives in the United States.

Below: Though uniform postal rates were established in 1845, two years elapsed before the necessary legislation was passed enabling the Postmaster-General to issue stamps for general use. In the interim many postmasters produced their own stamps. One of the crudest – and rarest – was that produced by James Buchanan, postmaster of Baltimore, Maryland.

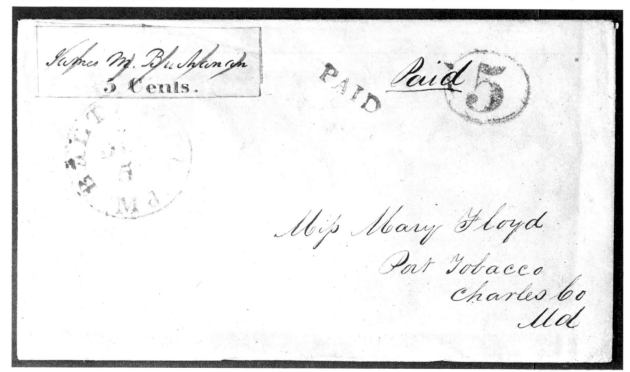

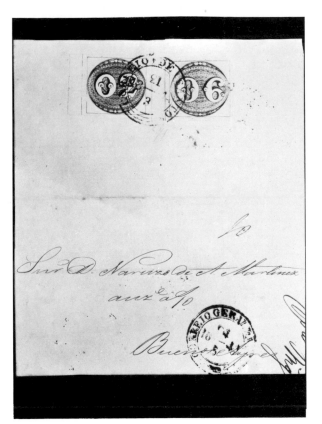

Brazil was the first country, after the United Kingdom, to produce stamps for nationwide use. The 30, 60 and 90 reis stamps of 1843 were known as "bull's-eyes", from their curious circular design. They were superseded a year later by smaller stamps known as "goat's-eyes".

POSTAL STATIONERY

Adhesive postage stamps were not the only method of indicating the prepayment of postage and from the outset many countries favoured various types of stamped stationery. In Britain, for example, there were envelopes, wrappers and letter sheets with devices printed on them to denote prepayment. These items, together with postcards and letter cards, are known collectively as postal stationery. Let us briefly consider each type.

ENVELOPES

After its unfortunate experience with the Mulready envelopes, Britain introduced a new type of stamped envelope on January 29, 1841. The envelopes were made of white paper and were sold ready-made and folded for use. An oval stamp was embossed in relief in the top right-hand corner, across which ran two parallel lines of fine silk thread embedded in the paper as a security device. These threads were of light blue and yellow respectively. The embossed stamp was printed in various colours – pinkish brown for the one penny, light blue for the two pence – and bore the profile of the crowned queen. The stamps did not bear the date of issue on them.

Stamps were issued in the 1850s by several states of the Argentine Confederation, but general issues appeared in 1858 with a sun emblem. The 5 centavos denomination is shown here on a cover from Santa Fe. Note the oval "Franca" (paid) postmark.

Right: 10-kopek stamped envelope from Helsingfors (Helsinki) to Wiborg (Viipuri) in June 1847. Stamped postal stationery was introduced in Finland ten years earlier than adhesive postage stamps.

A cover of 1848 bearing the curious circular stamp devised by William B. Perot, Postmaster of Hamilton, Bermuda. The stamp consisted of the Hamilton postmark, with the date-plugs removed, and the words "One Penny" and Perot's signature added. Orthodox adhesive stamps were not introduced throughout Bermuda till 1865. The Perot stamp now ranks as one of the world's greatest rarities. No examples came to light until 1897, and since then only a few have been found.

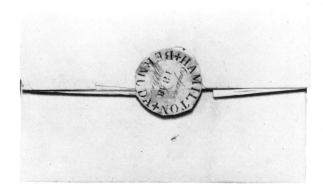

In 1845 the Grand Duchy of Finland issued envelopes measuring 114 mm. by 145 mm. The stamp, oval at first, later rectangular, was printed on the left and bore the arms of the grand duchy – a lion rampant on a field of stars. Many others followed soon afterwards. Finland, incidentally, did not adopt adhesive stamps until 1856. The design and style of stamped envelopes varied greatly. Some envelopes had a watermark – a dove carrying a letter (Switzerland), a triple-towered castle (Hamburg), an eagle (Russia) or a monogram (United States). In some cases the stamp was applied over the flap of the envelope; Austria, Japan, Ceylon, Mauritius and British India were among the countries which favoured this style.

WRAPPERS

Bands for enclosing newspapers are not quite as old as stamped envelopes. The earliest examples were introduced in the United States of America at the end of 1857. New South Wales adopted them in 1864 and Germany four years later. France did not issue newswrappers till 1882. The popularity of this form of stationery has declined everywhere in recent years, possibly because major newspapers are now distributed by their publishers all over the world.

LETTER-CARDS

Invented by Akin Karoly, the first letter-cards were sold in Belgium on December 15, 1882. Uruguay and Brazil adopted them the following year, Mexico in 1884 and both Austria and France in 1886. They consisted of stamped sheets of stiff paper or card, folded over and sealed round the edges. In most cases the edges were perforated so that the border could be detached to open the letter-card. Rare examples, from Newfoundland, contained miniature letter-cards so that the addressee could send a reply.

POSTCARDS

Dr. Emmanuel Herrmann, professor of national economy in the Military Academy of Wiener Neustadt, published in the *Neue Freie Presse* of July 6, 1869 an article proposing a method of correspondence consisting of a sheet of card bearing a printed stamp on the address side and reserving the other side for the message.

Baron A. Maly, the Director General of Posts in Austria, approved this idea and thus, on October 1, 1869, the *Korrespondenzkarte* came into being. Stamped postcards were released simultaneously in Hungary. In 1870 Germany introduced a stamped postcard in the French districts invaded by German troops, some

Left: Embossed stamps have been a feature of postal stationery since 1841. This early Canadian example also bears a 1 cent "Small Queen" adhesive stamp. Note the "killer" postmark, made from an old cork. Cork cancellations of this type were common in Canada and the United States in the nineteenth century.

Below, left: An example of the ornate stamped postcards in use at the turn of the century. This card, from Haiti, bears the postmark of a Dutch shipping line, January 16 and 18 1902, and a New York postmark with the words "for bch" (the forwarding branch).

Following on the vogue for Mulready caricatures, pictorial envelopes were popular in Victorian England, and many of them were elaborately hand-drawn and painted. This example, from Margate in 1886 to a soldier serving in Egypt, illustrates the hazards of soldiering on the banks of the Nile!

45,000 being released by the Berlin office on July 1 of that year. Great Britain began issuing stamped post-cards on October 1 (of the same year) and within six months was selling them at the rate of 1,500,000 a week! In 1872 there were only two countries which had *not* introduced postcards – France and Turkey.

In Paris, at the National Assembly, it was a Polish refugee named Louis Wolowski who intervened and by flattering the patriotic spirit of the deputies, suc-ceeded in getting postcards adopted; they were issued on January 1, 1873. Because of technical difficulties the first day of issue was delayed till January 15. Be-tween that date and January 24 no fewer than 7,412,700 postcards were sold in France. In 1878 the Universal Postal Union standardized the international tariffs for the circulation of postcards.

Many people found this novel method of corres-pondence rather alarming. They were shocked at first to see the text of a message laid bare for all to read, for letters were traditionally secret. Wisely, the the Austrian postal authorities printed on their cards: "The Administration does not accept any responsi-sibility for anyone concerned with the contents of this communication". Incidents, however, occurred.

In a little village in Normandy, three weeks after the first French postcards went on sale (February 6,

Pictorial envelopes also served a more serious purpose. Valentine of Dundee produced pictorial envelopes as part of the national temperance campaign against the evils of alcohol.

Right: Part of an envelope bearing a French colonial stamp used in Papeete, Tahiti, in March 1903. The majority of the French colonies used stamps of standard designs, only the inscription being altered to suit each territory.

Pictorial envelopes were also produced by Barnabas Bates, the American postal reformer, who championed the cause of cheap ocean postage to bring the English-speaking peoples closer together. This example, published by the New York Cheap Postage Association, was posted in London and addressed to Rowland Hill.

1873), a postwoman in charge of the counter read – before postmen and other witnesses – the text of a postcard which the Curé of Macey, the Abbé Cluché, had written to a lady! She even made a copy of the message, she found it so spicy. After a law-suit, however, the over-inquisitive postwoman was convicted and fined for violation of official secrets.

Official stamped postcards did not have a picture but confined themselves to inscriptions connected with the postal service. Certain postcards, however, were employed for private publicity purposes and some have survived that were used to give more important information, such as those of the siege of Strasbourg in Alsace. The city was besieged by the Germans from August 13 to September 28, 1870 and during that time was cut off from all contact with the outside world. The Strasbourg Committee of Aid to the Wounded sent a delegation to the German commander, General Werder and, with the help of the Swiss Red Cross, obtained permission to send out of the town special postcards giving news of the beleaguered inhabitants. The cards flooded into the sorting office in the rue de la Mesange but very few ever got through to their destination. After the surrender of the town the mail-bags were discovered in the casemates of the fort and were burned.

PNEUMATIC POSTCARDS

Several cities have at various times made use of a network of pneumatic tubes for the transmission of messages, and these have included London, Vienna, Berlin, Paris, Marseilles and Rome. At certain times, and especially in the early years of this century, special postcards, with or without a reply card attached, lettercards and envelopes were produced in connection with this service.

ENVELOPES FOR POSTAL PROPAGANDA

In many countries private individuals and societies have produced fancy envelopes for publicity purposes. Pictorial envelopes had their origins in the parodies of the Mulready envelopes of 1840, but the idea was later embraced by the Temperance Movement to illustrate the evils of alcoholism. The most desirable type of pictorial stationery for collectors, however, consists of envelopes produced by the Association for Ocean Penny Postage.

Elihu Burrit, born in New Britain, Massachusetts on December 8, 1811, was apprenticed by his father at the age of fourteen to a blacksmith. During his leisure time he educated himself and acquired a knowledge of many languages. (He subsequently became widely known as "the learned blacksmith".) He took an active interest in many of the burning questions of his time – temperance, international peace and the abolition of slavery. In 1846 he came to England where he founded the League of Universal Brotherhood. In 1851 he began a campaign in favour of the reduction in the cost of carrying letters between countries. The Association of Ocean Penny Postage recommended that each time a letter went from one port to another, it should only cost one penny, or its equivalent value. Thus it was immaterial from which town in Britain a letter was sent or to which town in, for example, the United States, it went. This scheme envisaged three stamps, inscribed "1 penny British Inland", "1 penny Ocean Transit" and "1½ pence U.S. Inland". To minimize complications, the Association proposed the use of special envelopes imprinted with stamps and illustrations for the furtherance of the scheme.

Many of these printed envelopes have survived. On one there was a picture of a steamship with the inscription "Ocean Penny Postage" on its sail. The envelope was also inscribed "The world awaits Great Britain's greatest gift – ocean penny postage" and "to make home everywhere and all nations neighbours". These envelopes were sold at 18 pence for 100. On another type of envelope there was a steamer with the legend "An Ocean Penny Postage is wanted by the world and will be a boon to England" and "all ports will open up, friends will greet the happy arrival and there will be no more enemies". On a third type of envelope a seaman flourished a banner with the words "Britain! bestow this boon, and be in blessing blest – Ocean Penny Postage will link all lands with thee in trade and peace". A fourth represents the ocean, with trains and chariots; the Ocean Postage stamp is on the left, while a space is provided on the right for the postage stamp of the country of the sender. Finally another proclaims "One penny would link in trade and peace the Brotherhood of Man. Blessed are the peace-makers God hath made of one blood all nations of men". This envelope is decorated with scenes from America, Africa, Asia and Europe.

Another postal propaganda card was distributed in France in 1905 by the newspaper *Le Matin*. It bore the printed address "To the President of the Chamber of Deputies at the Palais Bourbon, Paris" and the text "We demand that the charge on letters under 15 grammes should be reduced from 15 centimes to 10 centimes". On the reverse side, under the heading "European postal rates", appeared the postage stamps of Germany, Austria, Hungary, Belgium, Britain, the Netherlands, Luxembourg and Switzerland with an indication of the cost of postage. In place of the French stamp was a statement that it was the dearest of the postal rates. This petition was largely responsible for the success of the campaign for cheaper postage.

Regular services by paddle steamer were established on the great rivers of the United States in the early nineteenth century. This engraving shows a paddle boat on the Ohio river in the civil war period.

3
The post on water

At the beginning of this book we saw the various methods adopted in different civilizations throughout the world for the carriage of mail on foot, or by horse. In countries with navigable waterways, mail, like other things, was carried by boat and the water posts, both inland and marine, are an important part of postal history.

THE RIVER POSTS

In ancient Mesopotamia there was an intensive river traffic for many centuries along the Euphrates and the Tigris, using little boats made of reeds sealed with pitch. Letters, both official and private were undoubtedly among the merchandise they carried.

The first wooden boats were constructed in Egypt, usually out of acacia, sycamore or fir; cedar was used for sacred barges. The Nile has always been an important and reliable artery. A horse cannot carry more than about 100 kg. on its back, but if it tows a vehicle along an unsurfaced roadway (as all roads were in ancient times) it might transport as much as 600 kg. By contrast, however, a horse could draw a barge along a waterway with a displacement of 30,000 kg.! In 1776, Adam Smith calculated that on the route between Edinburgh and London a boat handled by six or eight men could carry the same weight as fifty carts driven by a hundred men and drawn by 400 horses.

The Romans were past masters in the art of water transport and in Italy and France they established a network of waterways of quite extraordinary density. Letters were often entrusted to merchants and travellers on these waterways and the Latin writers frequently mention the arrival of news carried by such messengers.

At the same time, at the other end of the world, Chinese engineers constructed vast networks of irrigation ditches and canals which were often navigated by small canoes. Many of these water-courses would not have been considered navigable by European standards. Very much later, in the fourteenth century, in Holland, the country best known for its inland waterways, the system of locks and sluices was first

For many years the river network of Peru provided the only means of communication. Letters were often carried by powerful swimmers where navigation by canoe was dangerous or impossible.

Right: Steamers on the Gambia River are equipped with their own postal facilities, including distinctive postmarks. This registered cover of December 1947 shows the label and cancellation of the T.P.O. (Travelling Post Office) No. 2 on the Gambia River.

adopted, offering limitless possibilities for inland navigation. If we describe these canals as trade ways, it gives some idea of their importance. Before the days of trains and aircraft most bulk transport was carried by boat. For centuries before roads were developed, waterways provided a quick and safe means of transport and to this day there are large parts of Africa and South America where the rivers make good the deficiencies of roads and railways.

Next to the tow-rope and the canal lock the greatest landmark in the evolution of water transport was the invention of the steam engine. After many unsuccessful attempts, an engine was eventually designed which could be adapted to the propulsion of boats without sails or oars. On September 24, 1707 Denis Papin experimented with a prototype for a boat propelled by steam. He went down the Fulda river from Cassel to Münden without incident, and later intended to cross to England where he hoped to perfect his machine. Unfortunately the boatmen of Münden were afraid that the new machine would take away their jobs, and they destroyed it. Discouraged, Papin abandoned the project.

In 1765 James Watt devised a greatly improved

steam engine which led to the first practical steamboat, sailed by Patrick Miller on Dalswinton Loch in 1789 and followed by Henry Dundas's steamboat *Charlotte Dundas* (1801-2) which operated on the Forth and Clyde Canal. Subsequently Henry Bell operated the steamboat *Comet* at Helensburgh on the Firth of Clyde. In the United States Rumsey was partially successful, and Fitch piloted a form of steam boat on the Delaware between Philadelphia and Trenton in 1790, though it was wrecked soon afterwards.

Robert Fulton was the first person to be really successful. After a brilliant demonstration on the Seine near Paris he made a triumphant voyage in the *Clermont* on the Hudson river from New York to Albany in 1807. A company was formed to secure a regular steamboat service between the two cities. Subsequently services were established on the Ohio and Mississippi rivers and since then all the great rivers of the world have been navigated by steamers.

In Europe the *Caledonia* was steaming on the Rhine at Coblenz in 1817, later came the *Nederlander*, then the *Concordia*, which plied between Cologne and Mainz. The Prussian-Rhenish Steamship Company was founded at Cologne in 1825. In Belgium, the Netherlands and Russia steamships were soon carrying mail wherever they went.

In 1839 the Royal and Imperial Society for Navigation by Steamship on the Danube and its Tributaries was formed. Roads in the Balkans were still rare and hazardous at that time, and the Society built steamers capable of navigating the dangerous Kazan Gorge and the Iron Gates, going as far upstream as Austria and downstream to the coast of the Black Sea. They also used the tributaries of the Drava, the Sava and the Tisza. At the end of the century the company possessed no fewer than 186 steamships and 727 tugboats. It took over Bavarian and Hungarian steamship companies and by 1883 its ships were travelling thousands of miles and carrying millions of passengers a year. Special stamps inscribed *Donau Dampfschiffahrt Gesellschaft* were used on mail carried by the company's ships from 1866 to 1874. Several other steamship companies had their own stamps and it is interesting to note that the first stamp issued in a British colony was that produced in Trinidad in April 1847 for use on mail carried by the steamship *Lady McLeod*.

During the siege of Paris (1870–71) many ingenious schemes for getting mail in and out of the city were put forward. The most popular of these involved sending bundles of letters soldered up inside zinc balls, which floated downstream to Paris. The zinc balls are known as *boules de Moulins*, from the village of Moulins where the courier was based.

A letter carried by a *boule de Moulins*. The letter was posted in London in January 1871 and is franked with both British and French stamps. Note the PD (paid to destination) mark. The endorsement "par Moulins" was intended to deceive the enemy.

THE "BOULES DE MOULINS"

During the autumn and winter of 1870–71 the city of Paris was surrounded by German troops. The beleaguered citizens attempted to correspond with their friends and relatives in unoccupied districts by various ingenious methods. The balloon posts are well known and are referred to in greater detail in a subsequent chapter. But as well as the air, the Parisians made use of the River Seine, which crosses the city, to carry messages from the provinces to the besieged capital.

A certain M. Castillon de Saint Victor had invented a floating sphere of 40 to 50 centimetres in diameter. Inside was a clockwork mechanism which released a tricolour flag on the outside. If the sender knew the speed of the current he could calculate the time a sphere would take to reach the centre of the capital from the outlying district upstream. He set the clockwork, stowed the letters carefully inside the detachable part of the sphere, sealed it and hurled it into the river. At the appropriate time the clockwork mechanism released the tiny flag pole and the flag fluttered freely to catch the attention of watchers on the river bank. This ingenious project was not, however, adopted.

M. Baylard, a post-office clerk, proposed the use of

small, hollow glass marbles. Screwed-up letters were inserted through a tiny opening; the marbles were then sealed and launched in the river. Small, light and practically invisible in the eddies and scum of the river, they needed no more than a light net to recover them. Unfortunately the Seine in winter was full of ice floes and it was impossible to distinguish the marbles as they drifted by, so this scheme was likewise declared impracticable.

Not long before the end of the siege, there was even talk of a kind of miniature submarine. Its inventor began to build one, but he was too late: the siege was over. A fantastic project was also undertaken about the same time. This scheme relied on various types of chemical solutions which, when poured on to water caused different reactions. The colours they produced were intended to be used as a form of code for passing messages. The uncertainty of the chemicals, their quantities and climatic conditions rendered this scheme utterly impracticable.

One project, however, *was* adopted. Three technicians, Messrs Robert, Delort and Vonoven, invented zinc balls which could hold bundles of letters and then be soldered up. Their density was just right for floating at a reasonable depth in the river so that they could make the maximum use of the current. In size and shape they resembled a baby's head. On December 1, 1870 a gunboat left the quays of Paris and went upstream as far as possible towards the lines of the besieging troops. At that point M. Rampont, the Parisian Director of Posts, threw a zinc ball into the water and watched it float downstream, back to the point from which they had set out. The following day the ball was recovered with a fishing net several miles downstream. On December 7 Delort and Robert left Paris on board the balloon *Denis Papin* with a stock of *boules*, and after a flight of just over 100 miles, they made a descent the following morning in the unoccupied zone (the Prussians were less than four miles away!) in the department of the Sarthe. The passengers were taken to the French provisional government headquarters.

After many political difficulties permission was obtained to send the first *boules*. On January 4, 1871, Robert, disguised as a peasant, slipped through the German lines to the banks of the Seine and put his *boules* in the water. With great courage he made numerous clandestine journeys between the post office at Cosne and the most favourable spots on the river bank, until the end of January when Paris capitulated.

Robert did not succeed in despatching all the 40,000 odd letters which had come from all parts of France, to the metropolis. It is estimated that he entrusted some 20,000 to the river. So that the secret of the *boules* should not be revealed to the enemy the public was asked to address mail intended for delivery: *M. X . . . Paris par Moulins* (Paris via Moulins – where the courier was based). For this reason these balls are known as *boules de Moulins*.

But what happened to the letters? None of them is believed to have reached the city at the time of the siege. The Germans had stretched fishing nets across the river and thus effectively blocked the passage of the spheres. However, from time to time, perhaps when the river has flooded its banks, or it has been dredged, or when repairs have been carried out on its embankments or to the piles of bridges, a *boule* has been brought to light with its correspondence still intact. Since 1871 *boules* have been recovered on many occasions, notably in 1882, 1910, 1920, 1942, 1951 and 1954. The most recent recovery occurred near Rouen in 1968 – well downstream from Paris. A dredger named M. le Grevelle found a *boule* among the mud brought up from the bed of the Seine. It contained several hundred letters dated January 1871. The French postal administration took charge of the *boule* and its contents but the Tribunal of Rouen decided on February 22, 1972 that they should revert to the finder. He was enjoined, however, to keep the letters until 1998 in case the heirs of the addressees should subsequently turn up to claim any of them.

CANAL POSTS

It would not really be true to say that man-made canals have had a beneficial effect on the post. Europe's great canals – the Great Trunk Canal in England, the Eider in Jutland and those of Russia and Belgium – were simply not designed for the acceleration of mail. However, they have played a part in postal history: the Canal du Midi, for example, constructed for Louis XIV in France by Paul Riquet between 1687 and 1681, permitted – and still permits – boats to pass from the Atlantic to the Mediterranean. In the nineteenth century it was used by *diligences d'eau* (water-coaches) and in spite of having to negotiate about a hundred locks, these post-boats rivalled their land-bound counterparts in speed. It was not until the installation of the railways that this canal system was superseded.

Two major canals are still very important today, the Suez Canal and the Panama Canal. Both have considerably reduced the time taken for surface mails. It is interesting to note that shortly after the Suez Canal opened in 1869 the Suez Canal Company issued a set of four stamps to prepay the postage on mail carried by its steamers.

MARITIME MAIL

The various postal administrations of the world did not bother to organize regular services with overseas countries until the traffic warranted it. Official shipping lines were rare and only grew as international commerce developed. It would be impossible, in the scope of this book, to do more than outline maritime development and give a few examples from each period.

In order to communicate with the Pope in Rome the kings of France had always made use of a safe and regular route. In 1551 Pope Julius III ordained that all French couriers should be given aid and assistance. At that time the normal route from Rome to France lay across various Italian states, over the Alps, across Savoy and Piedmont. Because of the turbulent political scene these couriers often found it safer to go down the Rhone valley as far as Antibes and there take ship to Genoa. The ships they used were known as *feluccas* and their crew consisted of ship's captain, cabin boy

and ten oarsmen. Every week a boat awaited at Lerici in Italy the arrival of a horseman from Rome who would hand over the letters for onward transmission to Genoa and Antibes. From Antibes another horseman departed for Aix en Provence. These ships often set out in the dead of night, in order to avoid patrols of English warships and to slip past the battlements of the customs post on the cliffs of Monaco.

As well as coastal traffic, there were also, of course, ships on the open seas. Every merchant ship carried a mailbag in those days. The shipowners undertook this service free of charge and on arrival the bag was handed over to the post office at the port. Gradually, however, various organizations and middlemen appeared and made proper charges for their services, including the transmission of letters. These individuals were known as Forwarding Agents. Letters handled by them often bore unofficial postal markings and examples of these are now highly regarded by postal historians. Generally speaking the agent would group together all the letters for the same destination

into one envelope, which would then be entrusted to the captain of a ship. The captain would in turn hand over the bundle of correspondence to another agent and he would then forward the letters to the individual recipients.

In former times these agents used to withdraw the correspondence of private individuals or business houses they knew from the post office, pay the duty and, for a moderate fee, send them on to their destinations. Certain agents made this their trade, like Hudson's News Room and Foreign Ship Letter Office or Gilpin's Exchange Reading Room and Foreign Letter Office in New York. Others carried on business at the same time as lawyers, bankers and insurance brokers. Sometimes letters were endorsed in a way which showed how they had travelled: "Arrived at Calais under cover of M. Auguste Mancel" (1815); or "Forwarded by Feuillet Lallemand Sisters by the *Formosa* at Le Havre March 1, 1831" (on a letter from Le Havre to Bordentown, New Jersey); or "Forwarded by A. Capdevielle and Company, New Orleans" (on a letter from Mexico to New Orleans in 1843); or "Received by steamship and forwarded from Marseilles by Charles Peyron de Tideman" (Naples, 1841).

While official networks of communication remained unsafe, infrequent or non-existent, these services continued to function.

We have already mentioned the Merchant Adventurers' Post between France and England. In 1633 the English Postmaster-General for Foreign Parts signed a contract with his French counterpart. It

Left: Britain maintained a fleet of swift, heavily-armed packet ships and many of them were involved in spirited encounters with French privateers during the wars of the eighteenth century. This print of 1797 records the battle between the *Westmoreland* and a French privateer off St. Eustatia in the West Indies during the Napoleonic Wars.

Steamships were used on the cross-Channel service from the early nineteenth century. This print shows the *John Penn*, launched at Greenwich in 1860, and subsequently used on the Dover—Ostend—Calais run.

provided an express messenger on horseback from London to Dover, an English packet-boat and an English post office at Calais where the French couriers would take charge of the incoming mails. Subsequently other agreements of a similar nature were concluded. It is worth noting that until 1783 the English always insisted on the use of an English packet-boat and the transmission of mail in any other ships was expressly forbidden! In 1666 there were two mail services a week from London to Paris (taking 4 days), one a week to Marseilles (11 days) and one to Madrid (26 days). The journey from London to Venice took 17 days. In 1886 the post between Dover and Ostend was established and two years later the service from Falmouth to Corunna was inaugurated.

In 1767 a Spanish ship began a monthly service between Corunna and Havana and four times a year there was a link between Montevideo and Buenos Aires and Spain.

A mail service across the Baltic, between Sweden and Germany, was established in 1824. Between France and Canada there was nothing, up to the end of the eighteenth century, other than a single voyage each year. Letters were despatched from Dieppe with the spring-tides of March and arrived in the Gulf of St. Lawrence about eight or nine weeks later. The returning mail-boat left for Europe in mid-August. It is interesting to note that about this time ships began to adopt names denoting their postal activities, such as the *Postillion*, or the *Black Post-horse*, the *Blue Post-horse* and the *London Postillion*.

For political and economic reasons it took a long time to organize communications between France and the United States by official mail-boats. Indeed, the shipowners cast a jaundiced eye on the carriage of mail by postal vessels, which would have competed with their own lines. A recommendation of Congress in 1779 was quite ineffective, but in 1783 five corvettes were assigned to sail between the two countries, two being warships of the French Royal Navy and three having been captured from the English by French privateers. These ships were placed at the disposal of the postal service, the number of guns was severely reduced from several score to only four each and cabins for passengers were constructed.

The first of these ships, *Le Courrier de l'Europe*, left Lorient on September 18, 1783 but contrary winds prevented it reaching the high seas until September 26. It arrived at New York on November 30. The ship carried mailbags and also twelve passengers, including M. St. Jean de Crevecoeur (who was taking up his appointment as French Consul in New York) and Mr. Taxter, secretary to Samuel Adams, who carried in his baggage the original document of the

Treaty of Versailles – signed on September 3.

The second vessel, *Le Courrier de l'Amérique*, set out on October 15 and reached New York on December 12. *Le Courrier de Port Louis* sank on the night of January 19/20 in the ice off Long Island, with the loss of sixteen lives. It was by *Le Courrier de New York* that Lafayette made his third crossing to America, where he was given a triumphal reception in 1784.

The mailboxes contained about 1500 letters, and on arrival were handed over to the post office official. Arrivals and departures became less frequent. In 1785 there were seven voyages in each direction, while the following year their number decreased again. At the end of 1786 the king of France tried to reorganize the service and introduced 24 packet-boats serving the Windward and Leeward islands (in the Caribbean), Mauritius and Réunion as well as the United States. This ambitious project was as short-lived as the first, since ten voyages in each direction took over a year to accomplish. In July 1788 the packet-boats were sold by auction. The following year a final fruitless attempt to revive the service was made by the ships *Jean-Jacques* and *Franklin*.

Henceforward here, as elsewhere in the world, communications had to rely solely on the ships of commercial companies. It was almost sixty years later (1847) before a distinctive shipping line between the United States and France was revived.

The use of steamboats on rivers and lakes has already been mentioned, but for quite a long time navigation at sea continued to depend on sail, particularly on three- or four-masted clippers. In 1818, as a tentative beginning, the *Rob Roy* steamer crossed from Greenock to Belfast with a small quantity of mail. In 1821 six steamers were provided for the postal service between Holyhead and Kingston and between Dover and Calais or Ostend.

An invention which revolutionized steam navigation was the screw propeller. The idea had been mulled over for a long time: in Britain, in France, in the United States and in Sweden various inventors had toyed with the subject. After various attempts by Bushnell and Paucton the first efficient screw was perfected in England in 1836 by F. P. Smith. It subsequently broke up during trials. In France the engineer Frederic Sauvage had produced a propeller in 1832 but it did not catch on, and he went bankrupt. Eventually a naval constructor at Le Havre, named Normand, in association with a British engineer named Barnes, produced a little model with four blades. The French authorities had this screw fitted to the packet-boat *Napoleon* which became the first steam driven, screw propelled mail-boat and later plied between Marseilles and Corsica.

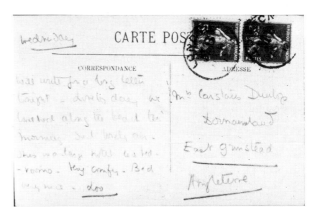

The cross-Channel ships had a movable box (*boîte mobile*) in which letters and postcards could be posted after the normal hours of collection. Special postmarks on both sides of the English Channel were used to cancel mail posted in this way, distinguished by the letters BM or, in English MB.

A cover from Warwick, Queensland to Tunbridge Wells, England posted on 1 October, 1873 and received on 24 November — seven weeks in transit. Note the endorsement on the envelope "Via Brindisi" indicating the route preferred. This letter would have travelled across the Indian Ocean, through Suez Canal (opened in 1869) across the Mediterranean Sea and overland from the Italian port of Brindisi.

A letter of April 1833 from India to England. The postmark "India letter Portsmouth" indicates that the letter was landed from a British ship at Portsmouth and subject to the special rate of postage levied on mail from India. Note the charge mark "Postage to London not paid", indicating that a sum of money was to be recovered from the addressee in respect of the postage incurred on the journey from Portsmouth to London.

Letter of February 1857 from London to Constantinople. The cross pattee postmark was applied in the foreign section of the General Post Office in London. Note the endorsement "Via Marseilles & French Mail" and the French transit mark "Angl. amb. Calais" (from England — Calais travelling post office).

Right: Before the opening of the Suez Canal in 1869, mail for India and the Far East had to travel either round the Cape, or make some of its journey overland between Alexandria and Suez. On the overland route, mail and passengers alike relied on camels to get them through the heat and dust of the desert.

A stamped postcard of 1880 from Springfield, Illinois to England. Note the cork "killer" of the American post office and the maritime postmark applied on arrival at Liverpool to indicate that the card was prepaid and carried by the United States Packet.

The nineteenth century witnessed a tremendous improvement in maritime mail. Throughout the world great shipping companies were founded in this period, and they relied on mail contracts for much of their business. In 1838 Samuel Cunard, a British shipowner, obtained a monopoly of the carriage of mail between Britain and the United States and created the company which still bears his name. In 1840 the *Britannia* left Liverpool and arrived at Halifax twelve days and ten hours later. About the same time the Peninsular and Orient Company (P. and O.) inaugurated their service via Suez to Calcutta, while the Royal Mail Steam Packet Company served the Caribbean area and the coasts of South America.

The British maritime postal service expanded rapidly to cover the oceans of the world. The Pacific Steam Navigation Company went from Panama to

Valparaiso; the African Company served the west African coast, the P. and O. covered the Mediterranean, serving Marseilles and Alexandria, and eventually extending its service as far as Hong Kong, Shanghai and Sydney.

The United States relied on the Atlantic and Pacific Steamship Company and the Pacific Mail Steamship Company for the mail runs between San Francisco and Panama and from New York to Chagres. Panama and Chagres were linked by a railway line in 1855, long before the canal was constructed across the isthmus. The Californian gold rush gave impetus to the development of maritime mail. The Oregon and California Steamship Company carried the mails from San Francisco to Oregon, Washington Territory and Vancouver Island, and as far south as Acapulco in Mexico.

In May 1847 the *Hamburg Amerikanische Packetfahrt Aktien Gesellschaft*, known from its initials as HAPAG was founded. Its postal fleet included the *Deutschland*, the *Rhein* and the *Nordamerika*. The Norddeutscher Lloyd Company also despatched mail-steamers to other continents.

The French postal administration developed a network of routes around the Mediterranean. From 1836 onwards its steamships, based on Marseilles, served the coasts of Italy, Greece, Turkey and Egypt. These fast new ships carried passengers as well as mail, and each had a crew of thirty sailors, two cabin-boys and thirteen stokers and mechanics. Later, French ships went as far as the Black Sea. The two leading French companies were the *Messageries Maritimes* and the *Compagnie Générale Transatlantique*.

The most romantic and famous of all the lines was the one whose mail-boats served the East Indies. Before 1839 the voyage from London to Bombay took

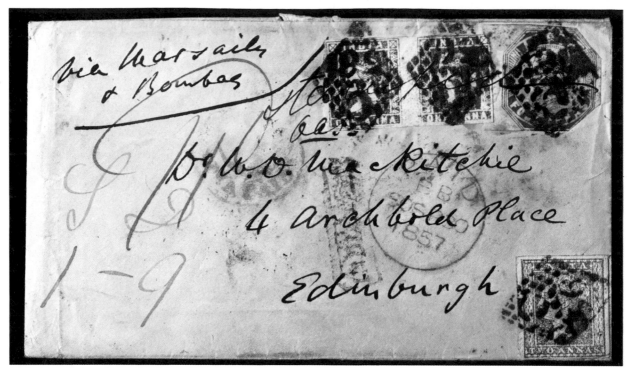

A cover from India to Scotland at the time of the Indian Mutiny in 1857. It bears a pair of 1 anna stamps and examples of the 2 and 4 anna stamps issued in 1854. The word "Stamped" was written across the stamps by the sender to prevent their theft by postal employees. The letter bears the endorsement "via Marseilles and Bombay" indicating its route.

Below: Coastal ships were important in the development of communications in many countries. This cover of the mid-nineteenth century from Antofagasta to Valparaiso bears an unusual ship postmark as well as the "Franca" mark of the Bolivian Post Office.

The Overland Mail had its twentieth century counterpart. A network of motor-coaches operated across the deserts of Iraq and Syria in the 1920s, connecting Baghdad with the Mediterranean seaports. This registered cover of 1927, from Lower Baghdad to Berlin, bears the label of the Overland Mail inscribed in English and Arabic (below). On the back (above) is the seal of the German consulate in Baghdad, and postmarks of Baghdad, London and Berlin.

Stamped postcard of 1894 from Bombay to London, bearing the transit postmark of the Sea Post Office through which much of the external mail of the former Indian Empire was handled.

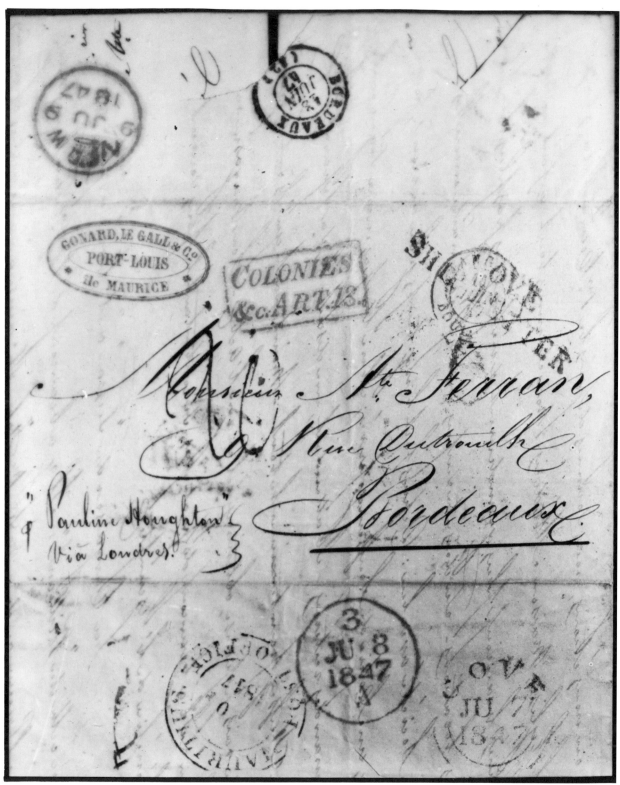

A pre-adhesive letter from Port Louis, Mauritius to Bordeaux arriving 13 June 1847 – barely three months before the celebrated "Post Office" stamps. The letter was carried on the ship *Pauline Houghton* as far as Cove in southern Ireland, where the Cove ship letter mark and date-stamp of 7 June 1847 were applied. Subsequently it went on to Dublin where it was postmarked 8 June, and to London on 9 June. The Boulogne entry mark was applied on 11 June, together with the "Colonies" explanatory mark, and finally it was back-stamped at Bordeaux on 13 June. Postmarking letters at each stage of their journey has enabled postal historians to trace postal routes of the mid-nineteenth century.

four months; it was a trade route of vital importance to Britain's economy and it ran for some 14,000 miles, via the Cape of Good Hope. The coming of steamers led to the establishment of a coaling station at the Cape. This route was, however, regarded as too long and inconvenient and in 1837 an attempt was made to send mail overland from Constantinople to Aleppo by special Tatar messengers. From Aleppo the mail was carried by camel to Baghdad but this last lap of the route was so uncertain and hazardous that the scheme had to be abandoned.

In 1839 the P. and O. obtained the right to carry mail via Gibraltar and Lisbon as far as Alexandria, a contract worth about £36,000 per annum. From Alexandria the mails and passengers journeyed up the Nile and the Mahmoudieh Canal as far as Cairo. From Cairo to Suez they went on horseback or on camels through the heat and the dust of the desert. It took about twenty hours to do a journey of less than a hundred miles. The P. and O. later improved the service by installing steamboats on the Nile.

Around this time negotiations were in progress between the postal administrations of France and Britain. They resulted in an agreement that mail would be sent overland from Calais to Marseilles by mail-coach (102 hours), and from there by French packet-boats via Malta to Alexandria (345 hours). The service began monthly and soon there were three voyages a month in each direction. From Suez to Ceylon, Madras and Calcutta the handsome ships of the P. and O., the *Bentinck* and the *Precursor*, took over the mail contract. Coal from Britain was transported on the backs of camels from Cairo to Suez and fuel dumps were established in the ports of the Red Sea.

In 1845 a British agent named Thomas Waghorn, encouraged by Germany, established a letter-forwarding agency in Alexandria. He hoped to prove that the mail from Europe could be greatly speeded up by routing it across Belgium, Germany and Austria, instead of France, and shipping from Ostend and Trieste. By this route mail could be sent from London to Trieste in $99\frac{3}{4}$ hours. The French opposed this scheme and by dismantling their mail-coaches and loading them on to railway trucks between Paris and Orleans and Roanne and Lyons, managed to reduce the time across country to 34 hours (Paris–Lyons) and 72 hours (Calais–Marseilles). Owing to the development of the nation's railway system, France was able to maintain this route, though with seasonal variations, until it was disrupted by the Franco-Prussian War of 1870–71.

The mails to India, which at first were carried in a sealed tin trunk, were speeded up in their journey across Egypt by the introduction of railways. The line from Alexandria to Kafr Zayat was opened in 1855, extended to Cairo the following year and to Suez in 1858. The railway enabled travellers to traverse the isthmus comfortably in 40 hours and superseded the Nile barges. In 1859 Ferdinand de Lesseps cut the first sod for his celebrated canal, which was opened ten years later. Henceforward mail-boats could travel all the way from the Mediterranean to India. Wars have closed the canal at various times, most recently the Arab–Israeli conflict, but it remains the principal sea route from Europe to the East.

SUBMARINE POSTS

The German submarine *Deutschland* was the first submarine to make a commercial crossing from Europe to the United States. Leaving Heligoland on June 23, 1916 it arrived on July 9 in Chesapeake Bay near Baltimore after a voyage of about 4,388 nautical miles. This was a considerable achievement for the time, especially since it meant breaking through the British blockade at the height of the war. The Wolff Agency, in an official announcement, stated:

"Regular communications with the United States have been re-established, the new submarines being able whenever they wish to carry not only letters, despatches and newspapers in defiance of the blockade, but also commercial goods. . . ."

The submarine left Baltimore on August 1 and surfaced in the south of the Weser on the 23rd of the same month. There was a second crossing in November–December 1916, from Germany to New London. Letters carried by this means bore an endorsement in German *Tauchbootsbrief* and in English "For the U-boat Deutschland" and examples of these covers are eagerly sought by collectors. Two German postmarks illustrate this heroic venture: one a circle inscribed *Deutsche Tauchboot-Seepost 1917* and the other a date-stamp inscribed *Bremen T.B. D.O.R.* (*Tauchboot, Deutsche-Ozean-Reederei*) and the outline of a submarine. Special stamps were provided for submarine posts during the Spanish Civil War and the Second World War. These, too, are eagerly collected.

MARITIME POSTAGE STAMPS

Usually ordinary stamps are used for maritime mail, but sometimes special stamps have been provided. In addition to those already mentioned the following should be noted. When the Suez Canal was opened the Egyptian government insisted on its exclusive right to issue postage stamps. In July and August 1868, letters posted along the Canal bore stamps of 1, 5, 20 or 40 cents, representing a steam

The notorious blockade runner of the Spanish Civil War, the *Girl Pat*, had its own stamp, showing the ship on a map of the South Atlantic. This unofficial stamp was not recognized by the authorities; note the cachet defacing the stamp "Returned from 'Girl Pat' as illegal Mail", and the endorsement "Contravenes Postal Regulations", applied by J. Reilly, Postmaster-General of British Guiana.

The island of Niuafo'ou in the Tonga group had a unique postal service: mail was taken to and from the island by a swimmer carrying the letters in a biscuit tin. The service stopped after a swimmer was eaten by sharks! The Tonga Tin Can Mail was noted for the many colourful cachets, applied in different languages, which adorn souvenir covers – such as this one, franked with the stamps marking Queen Salote's jubilee in 1937.

ship in full sail surrounded by a circular scroll with the words *Canal maritime de Suez*. At the time of the *Deutschland*, stamps featuring a lighthouse and a sailing ship were issued in Germany. In 1875 and 1879 Mexico levied a special charge on letters carried by sea in British ships for onward transmission to other countries. Special stamps were provided for this service and bore the inscription *Porte de Mar* (sea post), with the numeral of value in an upright design ornamented with arabesques. The service was discontinued when Mexico joined the Universal Postal Union and undertook responsibility for its own overseas mails.

In the same category was the *Drijvende Brandkast* (floating safe) of the Netherlands. Special safes were fitted to ships plying between Holland and the Dutch East Indies; if the ship sank the safes would float free and later be picked up. Mail carried in these safes was subject to a special fee, shown by special stamps.

THE COD-FISHERS' POST

Following the Treaty of Paris in 1814 the islands of St. Pierre and Miquelon were restored by Britain to France. The treaty provided, among other things, for the French to fish for cod off the coast of New-

Above, right: Letter dated 15 June 1921, despatched by "floating safe" from Amsterdam to Weltevreden; its 15 cent stamp shows a safe.

Right: Wreck covers are pathetic mementoes of great naval tragedies. The liner *Empress of Ireland* sank off the Canadian coast in May 1914 and the mailbags were not salvaged by divers till many years later, hence the sorry condition of the letters. The stamp on this cover has been washed away, oil and seawater stains disfigure it, but the cachet "Recovered by divers from wreck of S.S. Empress of Ireland" makes this an item highly prized by postal historians.

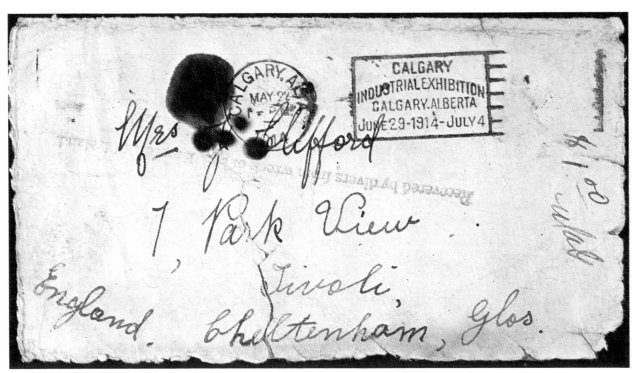

Cover from the Gilbert and Ellice Islands of Suva, Fiji in February 1939. The adhesive has been cancelled with the ship's mark of the S.S. *Triona* and the "Loose Ship Letter" cachet and date-stamp have been applied at Port Kembla, New South Wales in transit. Mail communications in many of the Pacific island groups depended on passing ships.

A Canadian stamp cancelled by the New Zealand Marine Post Office mark of R.M.S. *Monowai*, July 1937.

Tristan da Cunha, in the South Atlantic, is the most remote, regularly inhabited place in the world. Since 1952 the island has had its own stamps, but an interesting fore-runner was the so-called "potato" stamp, often found on mail from Tristan in the late 1940s. This registered cover bears the Cape Town paquebôt mark, and a "postage due" hand-stamp. The back of the envelope (not shown) bears two South African excess postage stamps, cancelled with a Johannesburg postmark.

foundland, in the Gulf of the St. Lawrence and off the shores of Cape Breton and Nova Scotia. Mail intended for these fishermen was sent out from France between March 15 and 20 each year and returned to France the following October. This always posed a difficult problem since the number of fishermen was usually very great. In 1914, for example, the French fishing fleet consisted of 226 vessels manned by 5,500 men, and naturally they wanted to write and receive letters.

Every time a ship returned, it would carry the mail for the others; consequently the collection and delivery of mail could take many months. Although the distance between the French ports and the fishing grounds was only 1,500 miles the voyage was anything but easy in the days of sail. The solution to the problem of mail-handling was provided by the French patrol-boats which kept watch over the fishing fleet. These patrol vessels went to North Sydney or Halifax many times each season. From these ports the letters were sent to New York, then to France via England. Thanks to the co-operation of the seamen of many nations the cod-fishers' correspondence travelled to and fro in very good time. The collection and distribution of mail on the fishing banks of the so-called "French shore", in the days before the advent of radio, was particularly dangerous and uncertain because of sudden gales and floating icebergs. That the mail system functioned so smoothly testifies to the friendship and solidarity of the fishermen.

Two examples of marine post markings
Below: Pictorial cancellation of the S.S. *Britannia* on the Göteborg–London route.
Below, right: Ship's postmark of the Norwegian M.S. *Hully*.

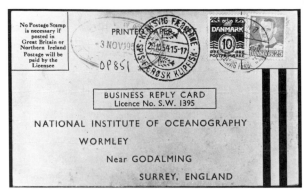

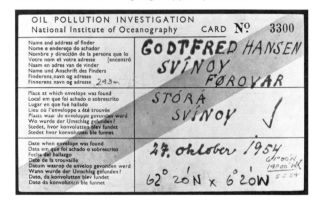

An example of the way in which "floating mail" is being used for scientific purposes. This card was one of several thousands dropped by the RAF in the North Atlantic to test the drift of ocean currents so that oil pollution could be accurately predicted. The cards were sealed in PVC, with cork floats. A reward of half a crown (12½p) was paid to each finder who completed the short questionnaire on the reverse (below). This example was recovered at Stora Svinoy in the Faeroes and bears the Svino and Klagsvig "kipper" postmarks.

A pictorial envelope showing a Dutch four-wheeled carriage, despatched from Breda to Amsterdam in 1866.

4
The post goes faster and faster

*I*N THE early history of the posts messengers on foot or horseback managed to cover surprisingly long distances throughout the world. Thanks to relays of horses, letters travelled quite swiftly and were very rarely held up on any part of their journey. As the volume of mail, both official and private, increased, it became necessary to improve the ways of carrying it. At the same time the mail systems were expanded to take charge of shipments of gold and silver bullion, jewellery and other small packets of valuables; important people, to whom time meant money, would also travel with the mails. Heavy merchandise was usually sent more slowly, by messenger. Gradually the state of the roads was improved and new types of vehicles were devised which made travelling faster and more comfortable. As in the territory served by the Thurn and Taxis postal administration, the transport systems were gradually perfected so that time was saved and maximum security was ensured.

MAIL-COACHES AND DILIGENCES

It was in 1784, in England, that mail-coaches first replaced horse messengers. In France, on the 22 most important post routes of the kingdom, letters continued to be carried by post-horsemen, but soon light vehicles known as *brouettes* were introduced solely for the carriage of mail. At this period there was a limited network of mail-routes covering most of Europe, offering relatively swift and commodious travel, but it was not until the nineteenth century that there was any appreciable improvement.

In 1815 John Loudon MacAdam was appointed Superintendent General of the Roads for the County of Bristol. MacAdam used his position to experiment with a new system of repairing and surfacing the roads. In October 1816 he treated eleven miles of roadway between Bristol and Old Down in a special manner and three years later found that, to the surprise of all the experts, the surface was still in a remarkably good condition. MacAdam had created a revolutionary process, which was simple and economic and which rapidly spread over the entire country, and eventually to other countries.

The departure of the Royal Mails from the General Post Office, London. England was the first country to replace horse couriers with mail-coaches. As road surfacing improved, bigger and better mail-coaches became common all over Europe, carrying both mail and passengers quickly to their destination.

An eighteenth-century post-house sign from Aarling, in Switzerland illustrates the continuing popularity of the liveried postboy as a symbol of the post.

The roads benefited by improvements of other types, particularly the increasing number of iron bridges. Abraham Darby built the first of these bridges over the Severn in 1779; in 1795 Thomas Telford erected another, and the iron-founders Walkers of Rotherham built a third. At the same time, on the other side of the Atlantic, James Finely invented the suspension bridge. In other countries engineers improved this type of bridge and adapted it for crossing ravines and valleys. For military reasons Napoleon I constructed the Simplon route and also that via Mont Cenis. In 1810, 17,000 vehicles used the Mont Cenis route.

By this time the would-be tourist could travel the length and breadth of Europe, guide-book in hand, and if he cared to he would undoubtedly observe the differences in the postal system en route. In Germany the postillions wore a uniform of yellow trimmed with blue, and a large hat embellished with the insignia of a posthorn. Across their chests was slung a bandolier from which hung a little trumpet whose noisy blasts made sure that everyone knew of their approach.

The wheels of the coaches required constant oiling; the toll-gates were numerous on account of the multitude of tiny states which formed a veritable patchwork across the map of Europe. Light, four-wheeled carts carried the mailbags and when the load was too great a second horse might be harnessed to help. The coachman was perched at the far end of the vehicle; the bundles of correspondence were stowed around him and the team of horses were constantly under his eye.

There is a story that about this time a carriage was seen driving through Munich drawn by two enormous wolves, trained by their owner. The police were called and the brutes were muzzled and led away. In Hungary the roads were very poor and dusty, but the horses were excellent. The postmasters sported long moustaches and wore a blue dolman trimmed with fur and silk lace. They had wolves to contend with too, but these were the wild variety which frequently attacked the post-riders.

In Russia "if one did not wish to trust to the posts one should seek to be accompanied by an under-officer who always found in his cane a means of urging on the postillions". The speed of the Russian horses with their large breasts and flowing manes was proverbial, while postal rates there were generally regarded as most reasonable. The post-houses contained three rooms: one for the passengers, one for the postillions and the third for the post office staff. The courtyard, surrounded with a neat hedge, made an ideal stopping place. Each coach-house maintained from ten to fifteen horses. A warm and cosy room was always waiting for the weary traveller. Travellers in the direction of Siberia were given a special kind of passport. The cord securing it was tied in knots, sealed with an official seal. The illiterate postmasters could tell by the nature of the cords and the number of knots which kind of carriage or cart and how many horses should be provided for each "client".

In Turkey primitive and uncomfortable vehicles rattled along at high speed, but the post-chaise which set out from Vienna went no farther than Adrianople. To get further, to Constantinople, a traveller had to bargain with individual horse-hirers for the journey.

In the Netherlands there were "water-coaches", drawn along the towpaths by horses. The *hijagerte* who rode the horses carried a trumpet made of cow-horn in his epaulette to warn the lightermen of his approach and get people to move off the swing-bridges. The punctuality of the service was said to be remarkable. By contrast journeys on land were made in unusual post-chaises. The horses were harnessed with simple cords to a block of wood which the driver steered with his feet; there were no shafts, and if he wanted to slow down, the coachman placed his feet on the neck of the horse and thus braked the vehicle on the downward slopes! Fortunately, hills are rare in Holland.

In Denmark a rudimentary telegraph system enabled the post-houses to get the horses ready at the next stage. The postillions carried a plan of the route which the postmasters referred to as they passed. In Sweden, before an official coach service was established, local governors were responsible for the posts and for providing carriages and postillions for it. In Spain, horses were rarely used, except as mounts. Mules drew the coaches, harnessed on very long reins which allowed them a great deal of freedom of movement. Skilful drivers thought nothing of hurtling over the mountain roads at breakneck speed – much to the alarm of the passengers. Conditions were much the same in Portugal, where the messengers travelled on the backs of mules slung with panniers of mailbags.

Italy's postal system developed in a similar way to those of France and Germany. The roads were excellent but sometimes, apparently, the postillions were rather tiresome. Fast, two-wheeled coaches were used almost exclusively. The coach was known as a *sedia* and the single passenger had to sit beside the driver. A peculiarly Italian practice permitted the hire of light two-seater vehicles for a fixed sum, a system known as *cambiatura*. In Switzerland the cantons provided a rapid and comfortable service which was an absolute model of its kind. The Nea-

politan posts were served by horses provided by the landowners whose territory bordered on the post route. They were allowed to keep back the profit for themselves but in spite of an obvious temptation to increase their profits, the mounts were usually of a very high quality.

In Britain almost 200 coaches were mass-produced to a standard design, to carry the posts. Spare parts were easily available and were speedily fitted in much the same way as motor car spares are today. The travellers found that the mail-coaches, developed by private enterprise, were comfortable vehicles capable of very long journeys and high speeds. The British were undoubtedly the leaders of the coaching industry and other nations copied them. The typical English mail-coach was a model of lightness and good taste. James Pollard's famous coaching prints show graceful "coaches and four" speeding across the English countryside. These vehicles did the trip from London to Brighton in four hours and took 42 hours to do the 400 mile journey to Edinburgh.

In France a person who wanted to get somewhere in a hurry had two choices: he could use the *malle-poste* or the *diligence*. The *malle-poste* carried the mail and one or two passengers. The traveller had to book a seat in advance, obtain a special passport, and

Left: A nineteenth-century Russian courier on a troika, travelling over the steppes. The speed of Russian horses, harnessed three abreast to a light, open carriage, was proverbial.

Right: Postboy of the Netherlands. Note the posthorn, universal emblem of the postal services.

Postal relay-stations across Russia provided the traveller with secure, if not luxurious stopping places.

French express mail-coaches gave their passengers a rapid, though probably a tiring journey. Travellers had to book in advance, obtain a special passport, and resign themselves to travelling day and night with a minimum of personal baggage.

Right: A Norwegian postman of the late nineteenth century. Note the carriole in the background and the large mailbag.

The United States Overland Mail crossing the prairies in the 1860s. The mails were frequently attacked both by Indians and by robbers, hoping for money and valuables.

A quotation from a guidebook of 1828 gives a good idea of the hazards of travelling "post" in Europe:

"Never shoot from a great distance with a pistol, but wait until the highwayman is near enough for you to see the whites of his eyes! . . . To protect yourself from the insects which infest the bedrooms . . . put the feet of your camp-bed in little vases filled with water as this cuts off all communication . . . Place at the disposal of your servant needles and thread and the materials necessary for kindling a fire . . . Never leave the door of your room ajar for more than a minute . . . Be satisfied with the local wine instead of asking for wine from a particular region, which is nevertheless taken from the same barrel."

THE RAILWAYS

A paradoxical situation arose at the beginning of the nineteenth century: at a time when mail-coaches went all over Europe, limited only by the speed of the horses, men had in their hands an immense, untapped force which could be adapted to transport – steam. Steam engines were in existence, but they were used to drive pumps, mills, printing presses and other devices in mines and saw-mills. Every day that passed saw some new development or some other way in which steam could be harnessed for new purposes.

Various attempts were made to adapt steam to vehicles but without practical success, and it was a long time before these prototypes were taken up by the postal services. In 1769 the Frenchman Cugnot constructed the first steam carriage, and there were experimental models in many countries, but it was not until the beginning of the nineteenth century that practical steam-driven engines were produced. In general, the roads of that period were not suitable for steam carriages. Later, attention was turned to a system using wooden rails, like those already in existence in mines and quarries. Metal rails were first used in the mines of the Coalbrookdale district of Shropshire and it was there that Richard Trevithick had the idea of building a locomotive to draw the mineral-wagons – the first practical engine of its kind in the world. In February 1804 his engine drew 10 tons of iron ore, 5 wagons and 70 men a distance of 9 miles. When he tried to draw 25 tons it was not the engine which let him down, but the rails.

Finally, in 1808, he built a circular iron railway near Euston Square in London. There he installed a locomotive called *Catch me who can* with a string of wagons. The railway was fenced off and he charged five shillings admission with a supplementary charge of a shilling for those who wished to ride inside.

The credit for establishing the railways on a com-

resign himself to travelling day and night with a minimum of personal baggage. In these express vehicles the mail could travel from Paris to Lyons in 34 hours (a distance of 310 miles), while the 171 miles from Paris to Calais took sixteen hours. The carriages paused only long enough to change horses. There were fifteen *malles* going to and from Paris and a further thirteen covered the cross-country routes. The other type of coach travelled at a lesser speed but was still faster than the ordinary methods of transport at that time. In 1814 they averaged 2 miles an hour, 4 miles an hour by 1830 and 6 miles an hour in 1848. The fares remained low, because a large number of rival companies competed for passengers. French postillions wore a blue tunic with red facings. They did not usually use posthorns, but cracked their whips with great gusto and used a variety of flourishes to show whether the customer was generous or not. They must have been particularly reckless drivers. In 1827 alone four thousand French diligences overturned or crashed as a result of excessive speed or overloading.

In the United States the Conestoga waggon reigned supreme from 1750 till 1813 when the Concord stagecoach appeared. The cinema later popularized Concord coaches as it did the coaches which Studebaker first made for the army during the Civil War.

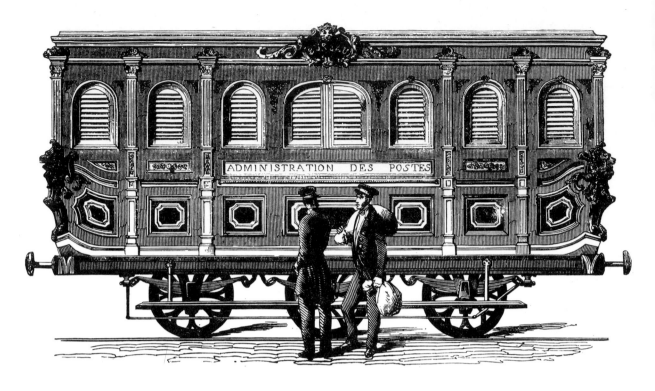

A French Post Office railway van, 1848. Note how the style of these early "sorting carriages" followed the design of the contemporary mail-coaches.

mercial basis must go to the chief mechanic of the Killingworth Collieries, in 1810. A self-taught genius, a passionate technician and an indefatigable worker, George Stephenson had all the qualities for success. His first locomotive was named *Blucher* and took to the rails in 1814. The following year he realized the faults in his so-called "Killingworth machine" and subsequently made a number of modifications. As late as 1825 he was still the only constructor in this field, a veritable pioneer.

He was not just concerned with developing steam engines for the mines. On September 27, 1825 the first passenger train made the run between Stockton and Darlington, a distance of 22 miles, and carried 600 people, most of them in coal-trucks but some also in the only passenger coach. Stephenson himself piloted his train, which was called *Locomotion No. 1*.

In France the brothers Seguin played an important part in the development of the railways, especially Marc, the elder brother. The first railways were those from St. Etienne to Lyons (1826), Alais to Beaucaire and Paris to St. Germain (1837), Montpellier to Cette (1839) and Strasbourg to Basel (1841). In France, however, the progress of the railways was relatively slow. In Belgium, on the other hand, the railways spread rapidly in all directions. On May 5,

Special postmarks are still used on mail sorted and franked in travelling post offices.
Above: The marks of the Norwegian Bergensbanen (Bergen railway train), 1966.
Left: Part of a Danish postcard showing the Hans Christian Andersen stamp and postmarks of the Rullende Post Kontor (travelling post office), 1936.

1835 three Stephenson locomotives, the *Arrow*, the *Elephant* and the *Stephenson*, inaugurated the Brussels–Malines route. In 1836 lines from Malines to Antwerp and Termonde were opened. In 1840, there were 201 miles of railway, linking the principal cities to Ostend. Because of its position in relation to the French and German railway lines, the Belgian rail network was very important. The earliest German lines ran from Nuremberg to Fuerth (1835), with Berlin–Potsdam, Leipzig–Dresden, Cologne–Aachen following shortly after. In Russia the railway from St. Petersburg to Tsarskoe Selo and Pavlosk was established in 1836, and the line from St. Petersburg to Moscow in 1837.

About 1838 the British post office concluded agreements with the principal railway companies for the carriage of mail by train. The Cheltenham mail-coach, for example, connected with the trains and each evening would run up to a special platform at the station to transfer the mails. The first mail-train as such, ran between London and Twyford during the night of February 4, 1840. It is interesting to note that this period was also the one in which Rowland Hill was making his important reforms. Fifteen years later the trains were fitted with special sorting tenders or carriages.

In France the first postal train was introduced in 1844 between Paris and Rouen. Previously the transportation of letters had been organized by the banking-houses on the railway between Montpellier and Cette in the Midi. The bankers entrusted a box of letters to the engine-driver who kept it on the tender beside the coal, but the postal administration, regarding this act as a violation of their monopoly, forbade it.

Gradually every country began to take advantage of the railways and, combining them with the mail-coaches, rapidly accelerated the handling and transmission of mail.

The postal vehicles then used, like those of today, consisted of two types: those which simply carried the mailbags and those in which postal staff worked. The first of these were notable only for the special security of their doors, the inscriptions, and the colour of the box. The second, however, were of a special design and usually in a distinctive colour. Those used in Britain to this day are painted a vivid pillar-box red. Inside they were fitted with tables, pigeon-holes and other equipment used by sorting staff. These special carriages were originally known as sorting tenders but are now generally designated as Travelling Post Offices (T.P.O.s). In Europe they are known as *ambulants*. As the mail-train hurtles

The interior of an American travelling post office, where letters could be picked up and sorted en route.

Below, right: U.S. Mail-train crossing the Sierra Nevada, 1870.

A greetings card for the New Year — and a new century — bearing the oval postmark of the Leipzig–Dobeln–Dresden railway post office. The inscription "MOSSEN 26.1.00 7–8N" shows that the card was posted at Mossen between 7 and 8 pm on 26 January 1900.

Letter from France to Madrid bearing the explanatory mark "Après le départ", indicating that it was posted on board a mail-train after the normal hour for the collection of mail, and the PD (paid to destination) mark.

through the stations the mailbags are picked up with a special apparatus and the contents can then be sorted out by the personnel on board. In the same way bags of sorted letters are dropped off the train at the appropriate point. In Britain they use an ingenious system of nets slung out at right angles to the side of the coach. A similar system was adopted in France. In the United States the train catches the mailbags, in passing, on a specially designed hook. Nineteenth-century engravers have left picturesque prints showing the dramatic way in which these mailbags were hooked up by trains travelling at speed.

Special mention must be made of the American postal wagons. A great deal of ingenuity was shown in the development of mail-trains in the United States. The locomotive itself played a very important part in the colonization of the virgin lands of America and in the subsequent development of communications. Train robbers were a major hazard and became so numerous that the railway companies were forced to devise a special coach. At the end of the nineteenth century, for example, the New York–Chicago route had "Burglar and Collision Proof Mails". These coaches had no communicating doors with the rest of the train and were armoured with

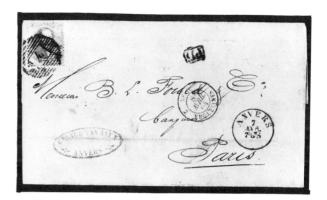

A cover of April 1864 from Antwerp to Paris. Note the PD (paid to destination) mark, the French entry mark — Belgium via Erquelines and, on the reverse, the backstamp of the French travelling post office, "Ambulant Est".

Examples of T.P.O. marks:
Top row: left, Amsterdam — Rotterdam Railway
              right, Kingdom of Württemberg Railway
Second row: Stamps franked "Late Fee Paid", Bombay,
              indicating transmission by railway post.
Third row: left, a mark from a letter travelling from La Tour
              de Carol to Ax les Thermes, France.
              right, White Nile T.P.O. mark, Sudan
Fourth row: left, Molsheim — Zabern railway post, showing
              the train (zug) number 21
              right, Aachen — Holzminden railway post, train
              number 30.

Russian out of town open letter of 1875, with the postmark of
the railway post, car number 51—52.

In the era before the establishment of the Universal Postal Union, the handling of international mail was very complicated. This cover of 1861 from London to Berg, Württemberg bears British stamps, a large P (to indicate that postage was prepaid all the way) and the circular mark "Aus England per Aachen Franco" (From England via Aachen, Paid). On the back are the transit marks of Cannstadt, Stuttgart, Berg and the Württemberg Railway post office.

steel plates and reinforced girders. Very thick panes of glass set in the roof provided light, while at night an excellent lighting system permitted constant surveillance. The personnel were provided with sleepers.

Thanks to various international agreements, mail trains were able to carry mail long distances from country to country. One of the best examples of this was the Trans-Siberian Railway. Begun in 1891 and built in stages, this immense railway had a postal service installed in 1900. From Moscow the posts went as far as Lake Baikal along the western shore by rail, then crossed the lake by boat or sledge depending on the season, and continued by train via Missovaia as far as Dalni (Dairen). On October 1, 1903 the line was opened to international traffic for the first time. Thus a letter from Paris destined for the Far East might catch Postal Train No. 125 leaving Paris at 8.05 p.m. It would go with the mail to Moscow, then on by the Trans-Siberian Railway, cross the Yenisei river on a bridge more than half a mile long, across Lake Baikal on the ferry-boat and arrive at Dalni twenty days later. From there the Chinese mail-steamers took two days to sail to Shanghai and a further two to go to Nagasaki in Japan. The Russo-Japanese War of 1904–5 caused

great disruptions to the line and to the handling of mail by this route. Dalni fell to the Japanese and Vladivostok became the terminus of the line. The First World War again disrupted communications. On the eve of that war a letter from Paris to Shanghai took 33 days by the ordinary route but only 17 by the Trans-Siberian railway. Admittedly the Russians levied a charge of 15 francs per kilo for letters carried on the latter route, and 3 francs for other articles (postcards were inadmissible), but the time saved usually made the charge seem worthwhile.

At around the same time the famous Indies Mail used a train which crossed France and Italy and saved much valuable time.

Nowadays aircraft have superseded the train as the principal means of mail transportation, just as the train usurped the position of the stage-coach which, in turn, had taken over from the horse-postman.

THE POST ADAPTS ITSELF

Wherever there were roads, the post used mail-coaches; later, wherever there were rails, they used trains. But in certain cases other forms of land transport, adapted to the situation, had to be used.

On January 28, 1854 Mr. Latimer Clarke in-

Right: A rider of the famous Pony Express which carried the mail from St. Joseph, Missouri to Sacramento, California in the 1860s. Like the U.S. Mail-coaches, the express riders risked attacks by Indians and robbers, as well as the natural hazards of difficult, newly-settled, country.

The first despatch of pneumatic mail from the North Western District Office, to Euston Station, London, 1863.

augurated a rapid system for linking up post offices. A network of tubes was laid down in London, along which small, cylindrical vehicles could run, propelled by air pressure. These cylinders carried letters and small parcels at great speed. A similar service was installed in Paris and Versailles and later in other cities. This was the pneumatic post.

Before the railway, the crossing of North America posed grave problems to the postal services: deserts, Indians, the Rocky Mountains . . . In spite of everything, a certain Major Russell dreamed up the idea of a postal service. He traced out routes, planned stages and formed the Pony Express Company (subsequently part of the Wells Fargo operation). The Company bought some 600 ponies of a small and hardy breed and recruited a hundred excellent horsemen to carry the mail. At each stage they would find a safe resting-place, a fresh mount and, in many cases a small troop of cavalry to escort them. Letters carried between St. Joseph, Missouri and Sacramento, California by Pony Express had distinctive postmarks and even stamps showing an express rider at full gallop.

In Canada and Alaska the companies engaged in the fur trade established trading posts scattered over the vast territory, often in very isolated situations, to which the trappers and Indian hunters could bring pelts for sale. Around these trading-posts there developed tiny communities, cut off from the outside world for much of the year. Until air travel became possible, the most important means of communication was by dog-team, and special envelopes were printed in Canada referring to it. Sledges drawn by dogs or reindeer are a very ancient method of transportation and dog-teams were already used to carry the mail quickly along the banks of rivers in Siberia in 1825. Five dogs could draw a person and his baggage.

The postman responsible for the distribution of mail in towns and their surrounding districts, also adapted various methods of transport to their special use. The letter-carrier on foot has survived from the Middle Ages to the present day, but bicycles became popular with postmen in the late nineteenth century, especially with those who had to take the mail to isolated farmhouses in the countryside. During the First World War pneumatic tyres were scarce and people had to ride on the metal rims. It must have been very uncomfortable – but deliveries continued.

In the years immediately before 1900 the petrol-driven automobile made its first appearance and soon speeded up the collection of mail from pillar boxes

all over the towns. Perched on his upholstered seat the driver bowled along at a steady 25 miles an hour.

In Belgium and in the north of France, the postmen used large mountain dogs to haul small, two-wheeled mail-carts along the straight, flat roads of the countryside. These little carriages lasted until 1914.

In every country where snow lies for long periods, postmen use skis. Not for them smart equipment, tapered ski-pants, chair-lifts or slalom stakes! Two slightly curved pieces of wood, one or two sticks, a thick scarf and a heavy cloak – and he was off. These skiers were not speed champions, but whatever the conditions, they covered enormous distances over all kinds of snow-covered terrain.

In mountainous country, with narrow, precipitous paths, the postman often uses an ass or a mule. These animals are not afraid of heights and are extremely sure-footed. The prize for originality, however, must go to the postmen of Landes. This French district, bordering on the Atlantic near the Spanish frontier, is noted for its marshy ground and the postmen got about on long stilts which enabled them to take enormous strides without getting their feet wet. When the postman delivered a letter the recipient had to get up on tip-toe, while the postman had to bend over as far as he dared.

Dogs have often been used for transport in difficult conditions. This nineteenth-century engraving shows them drawing a boat carrying a postman and the mailbags along shallow water at the edge of the river Yenisei, in Siberia.

A trade card produced on behalf of the Coolgardie Cycle Express which operated in the gold fields of Western Australia in the mid-nineteenth century. The special stamps and postmarks of this company are highly prized by collectors.

Left: The "hen and chickens", a form of pentricycle employed by the British Post Office in the late nineteenth century, to speed delivery of mail.

A stilt postman of the Landes, from a postcard published at the turn of the century. Stilts helped the postmen to move more easily over the marshy ground when they were delivering letters to outlying villages.

While Paris was besieged by the Germans, in 1870–71, it was impossible to send letters out by conventional methods. Sixty-seven balloons were released, many of them carrying mail. This letter of November 1870, inscribed ''ballon monté'', was carried on one of the flights, and arrived safely at its destination in Switzerland.

5
The air posts

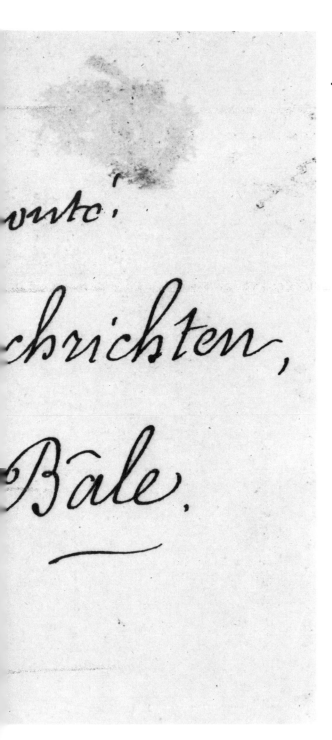

AFTER THE POST on the roads, by rail and by water, we come logically to the post by air. Today we take for granted the fast, jet-carried mails that take only a few days to travel from one side of the world to the other. But the first "airmails" were not at all like these. With their origin in ancient history, they reflect man's continuing preoccupation with the problems of flight, and his efforts to overcome his handicap of being heavier than air.

PIGEONS

In ancient times the Persians and the Arabs made use of homing pigeons for sending messages and this practice had certain advantages: rapidity, secrecy, directness and an easy passage over hostile territory. A post using swallows is said to have functioned in the Orient in antiquity. The snag about using pigeons is that they have to be taken to the point at which they are to be released and they only fly in one direction, towards their pigeonlofts. Until the First World War armies always had a section of "pigeon-fanciers" responsible for communications. Now that electronic methods of communications have improved, pigeons are used for racing, as a sport – though their homing abilities still make them potentially useful for carrying messages.

No account of the pigeon posts would be complete without a reference to the siege of Paris by the Germans in 1870–71, in which pigeons played an important role in postal communications. As soon as the French government realized that the capital would be encircled they took refuge further to the south, in the city of Tours. The Postmaster-General took over a number of pigeons on September 10, 1870. (A second batch of pigeons was intercepted by the Prussians and could not get away from the city on September 19 as planned.) This tiny reserve of homing pigeons was constantly replenished by fresh batches which arrived encased, two or three at a time, in small open-work baskets despatched by balloons. The first pigeon arrived at its loft in Paris on October 1, 1870. It carried an official despatch written by

The microfilmed messages carried by pigeons to Paris during the siege, were mounted in glass slides when they arrived, and projected by magic lantern on to a screen. Transcriptions were then sent to their destinations.

hand in tiny characters on tissue paper. The paper was rolled up into a very thin tube attached to the central tail covert of the bird and secured by a waxed silk thread.

By the end of October, thanks to Messrs. Traclet, Lafollye, Tasiers and Blaise, a photographic technique was being used to reduce the messages. The messages were written out on sheets mounted on card and a panel of these messages measuring 1 metre by 0·66 metres was reduced to a message 6 centimetres by 4 centimetres. This reduction in size made it possible to despatch a large number of messages. The postal administration allowed the public to take advantage of the system and in the course of a single month 10,000 messages were despatched to Paris. However, an even better method was to be developed. At the international exhibition held in Paris in 1867 one of the greatest attractions had been the demonstration by M. Dagron, of micro-photography. He sold penholders whose handles were pierced with a small hole, measuring only a few millimetres across. Looking into this tiny hole, you could see pictures of several hundreds of members of the Chamber of Deputies!

Dagron and his three associates, made a contract with the postal administration, and left by balloon

Pigeons were used for carrying messages from the very earliest times up to the First World War, when electronic methods of communications made them redundant. The message was attached either to the pigeon's leg or to one of its tail feathers, and the pigeon's unerring instinct led it direct to its destination.

Right: A Swiss letter-box of 1845 shows a "pigeon postman" — perhaps symbolizing the directness and reliability of the post.

for the provinces with their equipment. After a great many difficulties (one of their balloons was shot down by the Prussians) Dagron made rapid progress. Once the texts were reduced and mounted on minute *pellicules* of collodion, they were encased in a very thin tube which was again attached to the tail coverts of the pigeon. The reduction was so great that each tube could take between 35,000 and 40,000 messages.

The journey was not an easy one. It was in the depths of winter; the cold and the snow paralyzed the pigeons and many of them never arrived at their destination. However, a careful note was kept of each departure and arrival so that the lost pellicules could be replaced and a duplicate set despatched. More than 350 pigeons were used during the four and a half months of the siege.

In Paris, observers kept a constant watch for the arriving pigeons and as soon as they alighted they were relieved of their light loads. It is said that the pigeons refused to eat anything until they had carried out a lengthy and scrupulous clean-up, preening each of their feathers soiled during the flight. As for the pellicules, you can imagine how carefully they were unrolled; then mounted in glass slides, and, greatly magnified, they were projected by magic lantern on to a screen. Secretaries transcribed the different texts and these, both official and private, were then despatched to their destination in the ordinary way.

During the Second World War Dagron's old method was adopted again to enable American servicemen stationed in Europe to correspond with their families in the U.S.A. The soldiers wrote on sheets of paper of a standard type and these were then photographically reduced in size. The negatives were flown out to the U.S.A., where they were then despatched to the families. This sytem, inaugurated in June 1942 between America and Great Britain, is known under the name of "V. Mail" or the "Airgraph system". It enabled countless millions of messages to be despatched.

Pigeons have been used at various times, both in peace and war. The best known commercial pigeon posts were those which operated between Auckland and the offshore islands of New Zealand at the turn of the century. The "Great Barrier Pigeon Service Co." and the "Marotiri Copper Syndicate", both operated pigeon posts, complete with special stamps, flimsies and stationery, until the extension of the telegraph services rendered this method of communication obsolete.

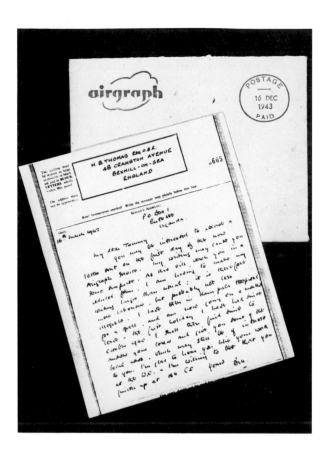

The microfilming of mail, introduced in the Franco-Prussian War, was revived in World War II by Britain and America. This illustration shows an airgraph, the photostat made from the microfilm, and the special window envelope in which the message was forwarded to the addressee. It was sent from Kampala, Uganda, then a British Protectorate, to England.

Right: A *ballon monté* letter flown from Paris by manned balloon. It left Paris on 24 November 1970, and arrived in London 8 days later, on 2 December. Thousands of letters were transmitted on this, the world's first official airmail service.

The launching of a balloon from the Gare du Nord, Paris during the siege of 1870–71.

BALLOON POSTS

The story of balloons is a marvellous one. The invention of balloons, at the end of the eighteenth century, captured the imagination and the ballooning craze rapidly spread across Europe and America. Hot air balloons were superseded by those filled with highly inflammable gas. Ballooning was pioneered by the Montgolfier brothers and Pilatre de Rozier. After de Rozier's tragic death, Blanchard and Jeffries in 1785 dared to cross the English Channel in a balloon. The first balloon post was created on January 9, 1785 by Blanchard when he "ascended in a balloon from the old prison of Philadelphia carrying a letter entrusted to him by Washington himself". More important, however, was the flight of John Wise in 1859 in the balloon *Atlantic*, carrying a bag of letters destined for St. Louis (Missouri). He got as far as Lake Ontario before crashing: nevertheless the mail was salvaged and forwarded to New York. In 1877 Archer King carried mail from Nashville to Gallatin (Tennessee) in his balloon *Buffalo*. In spite of these mail deliveries, ascents by free balloon continued to be regarded as a form of sport, aerobatics. Displays and first flights took place but no attempt was made to organize a regular airmail service by balloon. It

only needed a change of wind for the apparatus to start off in the opposite direction, and it was quite impossible to travel from one town to another at will.

The balloon seemed doomed to be a mere amusement until the Franco-Prussian War of 1870–71 demonstrated that it could be useful, if not indispensable. As we have seen, the blockade of Paris lasted from September 18, 1870 until the end of January 1871 and during this time, a balloon post was officially authorized. A total of 67 balloons left Paris under the noses of the Germans (fortunately anti-aircraft artillery was non-existent in those days) and most of them carried letters, 55 of which were from the postal administration. Some ascents were without incident, others were extremely hazardous and a few were fatal. At the beginning of the siege of Paris, a few balloons were already in the city, but subsequently the large majority were constructed in improvised workshops in the disused railway stations.

As there were insufficient communications by pigeon with Paris, an attempt was made to reach the capital by balloon. Theoretically the idea was sound. All that was required was to have inflated balloons ready to leave from a region occupied by French troops where there was a supply of gas. They only needed to wait for the wind to blow in the direction

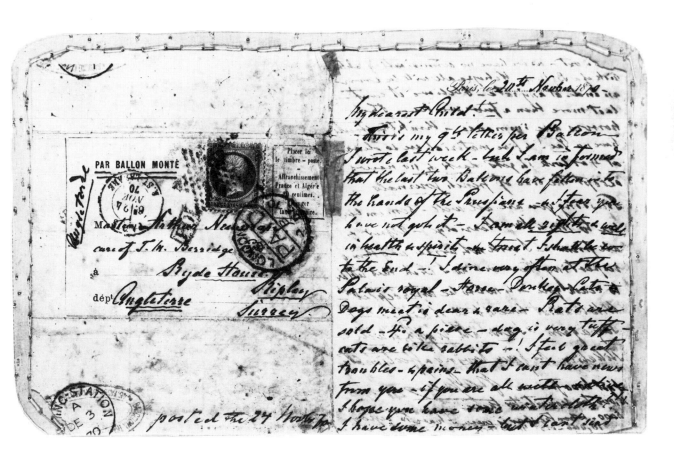

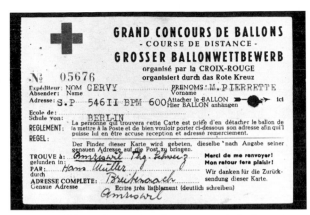

Balloon mail is used nowadays for stunts and charity projects. This card was carried on a balloon entered in a competition organized by the Red Cross in Berlin. It was found in Amriswil, Switzerland.

Left: A letter sent from the besieged city of Paris on 6 November, 1870 by the balloon *La ville de Chateaudun*. It is addressed to Rotterdam.

German Uhlan cavalry tracking a balloon during the siege.

of Paris and they would be off . . . Alas, it was not quite so simple a matter. Several attempts were made, but not one succeeded. With the capitulation of Paris the balloon post came to an end. Overall it had been very successful, though, like the pigeon post, it had only functioned one way.

Since then, at festivals, exhibitions and sporting events, philatelists have organized balloon flights carrying useless mail with special stamps and seals for publicity purposes. Special stationery, postmarks, labels and cachets have been produced and kept as collectors' pieces but none has the authenticity and charm of the letters of 1870–71 flown out of Paris despite cold, storm, the darkness of night or fusillades!

During the same conflict it is worth noting two experiences concerning mail despatched by air. In two besieged towns, Metz and Belfort, the encircled French armies succeeded in communicating with the outside world. Between September 5 and October 26, 1870, small balloons made of oiled and varnished paper were flown out from Metz. There was no question of them carrying more than a few little bundles of letters. Each letter was written on tissue paper measuring 5 by 10 centimetres, carefully tied up, with the address on one side and the text on the other. The despatches bore a label which asked the

person who discovered the frail device to take it to the nearest post office. This process was successful in many instances and the fragile little rectangles called *Papillons de Metz* now rank among the world's rarest airmail mementoes.

DIRIGIBLE BALLOONS

For a long time engineers had attempted to produce balloons which could be steered. There were many setbacks, due mainly to the weight of the motor and to its lack of power; the lack of rigidity of the balloons also impeded manoeuvres in high winds. In August 1884 the engineers Renard and Krebs made a flight in the airship *La France* and attained a height of 300 metres near Paris. This airship had a diameter of 8 metres and was 52 metres long, with an enormous propeller. The airship made a circuit of several miles but was only partially successful. In the early years of this century the Brazilian Santos Dumont made some tiny dirigibles which were highly manoeuvrable but were too small to be of practical use for carrying freight or mail.

The problems were finally overcome by the German cavalry officer, Count Ferdinand von Zeppelin. He succeeded in constructing immense metal skeletons, capable of flying under any conditions. These machines were used by the Germans in the First World War in bombing raids on Paris and London, but they proved very vulnerable. Some of them were shot down in flames, like the L21 (L = *Luftschiff*/Airship) in 1916.

After the war Germany continued with the project. In 1927 the L59 stayed airborne for 96 hours and travelled almost 5,000 miles.

The following year this airship, piloted by Dr. Eckener crossed the Atlantic. In 1929 it left Friedrichshafen on the round-world trip, via Siberia, Japan, the Pacific, North America, the North Atlantic and returned to Friedrichshafen. It was a triumph. From 1930 regular services were attempted, the most notable being the flight to South America (Rio de Janeiro), and to North America (Lakehurst). They carried freight, of course, as well as mail and passengers. By 1932 the Zeppelins had carried out 590 flights. The famous *Hindenburg*, measuring about 250 metres in length and 50 metres in height, was put into service. This giant exploded in May 1937, and was the last of its kind. Rivalled, then replaced by aeroplanes, the Zeppelins had covered millions of miles, transporting 52,000 people and several hundreds of tons of fuel and mail. Collectors

Right: The era before World War I witnessed aviation meetings all over Europe but especially in France. Special postcards, labels and even postmarks were provided for the occasion. This card was a souvenir of the aviation meeting at Betheny sur Marne in 1909.

The lonely South Atlantic island of Fernando Noronha served as a rendezvous point for the German transatlantic aircraft — the giant Zeppelin airships and the Dornier-Wal flying boats— in the 1920s.

of letters and postcards try hard to gather samples or souvenirs of test flights, crossings, and regular services of these famous balloons.

A host of "airship" stamps was issued by many different countries, and postmarks, cachets, envelopes and cards were produced as souvenirs of the different epic flights. They are in keen demand, and certain ones are very rare. The military flight covers of 1914–18 when Zeppelins were used, and postcards and postmarks associated with the pioneer flights of the Zeppelins before the First World War are also very rare.

AIRMAIL

After years of experiment, the brothers Wilbur and Orville Wright succeeded in making the first powered flight of a heavier-than-air machine at Kitty Hawk, in North Carolina in December 1903. There were many others who worked on the problems of powered flight – Stringfellow in England, Lilienthal in Germany and Ader in France. During this time Santos Dumont also worked independently on the problem and succeeded in making a flight of 200 metres at a height of 6 metres. This was the birth of aviation; in the half century that followed, it was to revolu-

tionize the whole range of men's activities. It goes without saying that the postal services benefited from this progress. Aircraft were admirably suited to the carriage of letters quickly over relatively long distances, but it took a comparatively long time for this to become accepted by postal administrations.

At first, mail was transported by air on the occasion of aviation meetings or for publicity purposes. These events did much to popularize aviation and are remembered today chiefly by their philatelic souvenirs. Special postal facilities were provided at many of these meetings and examples of the postcards, labels, semi-official stamps, cachets and cancellations are now highly prized by aero-philatelists. It should be noted, however, that very few of these items were actually flown and therefore do not fall into the category of "airmail" as such. Cards posted at Nantes in 1910, for example, were endorsed with *Par aéroplane*, though they never, in fact, left the ground. The postal services on the ground were still the true despatchers of mail. In the same year the Morehouse Martens Company instructed the pilot Parmalee to carry a parcel of silk from Dayton to Columbus, Ohio, and had cards printed to commemorate this service; this is regarded as the earliest example of aerial parcel post.

The first air mail route in the United States linked Washington, New York and Philadelphia. The planes, Curtiss JN—4—H bi-planes, known as Curtiss Jenny's, were specially modified to carry mailbags.

Right: Postcard dated November, 1930, sent by the airship *Graf Zeppelin* to Bussum, with the slogan postmarks "Luftschiff Graf Zeppelin. Fahrt nach den Niederlanden 1930" (Airship Graf Zeppelin. Journey to the Netherlands, 1930) and "Neergelated boven Venlo uit het luchtschip Graf Zeppelin 11 November '30". (Dropped over Venlo from the airship *Graf Zeppelin*). Mail was dropped from the airships in specially-padded containers with long, red and white streamers which helped watchers on the ground to track the descent.

In 1911 a Northampton (England) footwear manufacturer despatched several pairs of shoes to Hendon by aeroplane. Each parcel was "franked" by a special label provided by the manufacturer. Special postmarks were used during the same period on mail flown from Brescia (1900), Verona (1910), and Rimini. Publicity labels of the greatest rarity were also produced in Switzerland as part of the publicity campaigns for military aircraft.

The year 1911 was an important one in the annals of airmail service. At Allahabad in British India the aviator Pequet established the first official airmail service, letters and cards bearing a special pictorial postmark. The organizer of this service, Sir Walter Wyndham, subsequently organized an airmail service between Hendon and Windsor in connection with the coronation celebrations of 1911, and special postmarks and stationery were provided. On September 25 the United States Post Office Department flew out from the airport at Garden City one of the first machines carrying mail. The postmark was inscribed "Aeroplane Station No. 1" and a cachet "Aerial Special Despatch" was also struck. A second service was inaugurated on November 6 of the same year, the point of departure being Arkansas "Aeroplane Mail Service League Park Station Fort

Smith", according to the cachet used at that time. In Italy a return airmail service between Milan and Turin was established the same year, while in Morocco the newspaper *Petit Journal* was flown between Casablanca and Rabat and Fez.

From this point onwards, aeroplanes began to be more important. Though the First World War did nothing to encourage postal relations, the technical innovations it led to made commercial aviation more feasible when the conflict was over. Let us take several examples chosen from hundreds.

In 1916, the American Congress voted $100,000 for the creation of an experimental airmail service. This project was sponsored by Morris Sheppard, senator for Texas. At the beginning of 1918, thanks to the collaboration of Otto Prager, second assistant to the Postmaster-General, Albert S. Burleson, and the engineer, Captain Benjamin Lipsner, the first airmail route, linking Washington and New York via Philadelphia was devised. The army provided the aircraft, Curtiss JN-4-H biplanes popularly known as the "Jenny". They were powered by a Hispano-Suiza 8-cylinder engine and the cabin was modified to carry mailbags. On May 11, 1918 the Post Office announced that the service would begin on May 15 and would run daily, except Sundays. The rate for

letters was fixed at 24 cents up to one ounce. A stamp depicting the Curtiss was produced for the occasion.

It had been planned that one machine would take off from New York for Philadelphia (90 miles) and another from Washington to Philadelphia (128 miles). There, the two aircraft would wait and then take off again in opposite directions. The total flying time involved would be a little over three hours. On May 15, the inauguration day, Curtiss No. 38262, piloted by Lieutenant George Boyle was awaiting take-off from the polo ground in Washington watched by President Wilson and the Postmaster-General, accompanied by various dignitaries. The mailbags were loaded, the President handed over a letter addressed to the Postmaster of New York. Contact! The engine refused to fire. Boyle tried again, but in vain. Wilson became restless . . . and then it was discovered that the fuel tank was empty! There was no fuel supply at the polo ground so gasoline was pumped out of other aircraft nearby and transferred to Boyle's machine. He took off at 11.30 a.m. Upset no doubt by this incident Boyle flew in the wrong direction, away from Philadelphia. In a few minutes he was lost, and after trying fruitlessly to regain his course he came down in a field near Waldorf in Maryland. In so doing he broke a wing

and his propeller. The Washington-to-Philadelphia flight was abandoned for the day, but the following day Lieutenant James Edgerton, in another machine, made the flight successfully with 7,000 letters.

By contrast Captain T. Webb made a good take-off from New York and arrived according to plan at Philadelphia where he waited in vain for the arrival of Boyle's Curtiss! From Philadelphia two other Curtiss biplanes took off, one setting out for New York (without the Washington mail) and the other for Washington. Thus the first line was in service and functioned with great success.

In June 1918 attempts were made to establish a return service between New York and Boston but this failed owing to extreme conditions. This link was quickly abandoned. The "Jenny" was superseded on Monday August 12, 1918 by civil aircraft of a more modern design. The Standard JR 1-B biplanes could reach a speed of 100 m.p.h. and they provided an excellent service.

The first flight between New York and Chicago was difficult. On September 5, 1918 two machines took to the air at Belmont Park. One was piloted by Max Miller and the other by a flier named Gardner; their flights were 1 hour 40 minutes apart.

The first, Miller's, was hampered by bad visibility

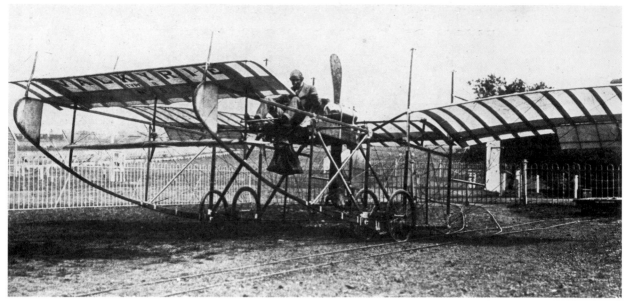

Britain's first official airmail was the United Kingdom Coronation Aerial Post of 1911. Flights by flimsy aircraft such as this were staged between London (Hendon) and Windsor to celebrate the coronation of King George V.

A card flown by the "aerial postman" of the Coronation Aerial Post. Special postmarks were used at both Hendon and Windsor and envelopes and postcards, in various colours, depicted Windsor Castle.

Right: Loading the night mail, Los Angeles 1929.

and Miller had to come down at Danville (Pennsylvania) where he asked the way and then flew on to Lock Haven, the first stage of the flight. From there he flew to Cleveland, but a leak in the radiator forced him to land in open country where an angry farmer held him up at gunpoint, refusing to listen to any explanation! The luckless Miller had to take off without water and land again after a short spell. After a lucky repair he finally reached Cleveland where he again landed to find out his position. The following day he arrived at Chicago via Bryan at 6.55 p.m.

The second plane also suffered serious mechanical trouble and was prevented from flying by bad weather. It did not reach Chicago until two days later. On their arrival the aviators were given a tremendous reception by the waiting crowds.

On the return flight, Gardner made no stops and reached New York after dark. He was unable to locate the airfield and came down at random, destroying his Curtiss R.4. Nevertheless he had made the first night-flight and also beaten the record for rapid communication between the two cities. Other flights between New York and Chicago were made the following year.

The network of air routes expanded greatly after the war. In 1920 attempts were made to link Key West in Florida and Cuba, and also San Francisco and Los Angeles. In 1921 a complete night-flight took place on one part of the New York–San Francisco route (from North Platte to Chicago). This journey across the continent took a little over 24 hours, a vast improvement over the four or five days taken on the train journey. After this, increasing use was made of internal airmail for linking the towns and cities of the United States.

The first European airmail company was established in Denmark (the *Danske Luftfart Selskab*), and the first regular airmail service was initiated by the *Deutsche Luft Reederei* between Berlin, Leipzig and Weimar in February 1919. A few weeks later aeroplanes of Aircraft Transport and Travel Ltd. were operating between Paris and London.

Certain countries with difficult terrain looked to postal avaiation for a solution to their problems. In Colombia an internal air service was inaugurated on June 18, 1919 and mail was flown using a stamp overprinted for the occasion. Only 189 examples of this stamp were produced. In 1920 the *Compania Colombiana de Navegacion Aerea* was formed and issued labels which rank among the most picturesque ever produced for this purpose. They show various bi-

Right: This cover is addressed to Mrs. Elsie Moseley, sister of Sir John Alcock. He wrote to her from Newfoundland and then carried the letter with him on his epic flight. Note the special $1 stamp provided by the Newfoundland authorities for this occasion.

Cover bearing the special air stamps of the Colombian SCADTA airline. Special stamps and stationery were used by SCADTA from 1919 to 1931, when the service was nationalized.

The most unusual air stamps were those used by the CC de NA (Compania Colombiana de Navegacion Aerea) in 1920. These consisted of trade cards printed on gummed paper, suitably overprinted and surcharged.

A rare flown cover from the Universal–Dr Fanck Expedition, Greenland in 1932, bearing the hand-printed airmail stamp of Rockwell Kent and a Danish stamp, postmarked on arrival at Copenhagen.

planes flying over different views of the countryside. In Equador on November 4, 1920 the Italian aviator Lint flew from Guayaquil, the chief port, to Cuenca in the high Andes, in the biplane *Telegrafo I.* On November 28 he flew from Riobamba to Quito. On July 5 1930 the airline Equador–Guyanas was established providing a link, via Colombia and Venezuela, with Paramaribo in Dutch Guiana.

In French Guiana the main obstacle to communications were the vast tropical rain forests, intersected by rivers and waterfalls which had to be negotiated by canoe. The journey from Cayenne to the territory of Inini took three weeks. In 1921 the T.A.G. (*Transports aériens guyanais*) was authorised to carry mail by sea-plane in addition to the normal freight and immediately reduced the travelling time to eight or ten hours. Local vignettes were printed, one featuring the head of Mercury somewhat crudely engraved in wood by a convict (Cayenne was at that time a prison). After some months the airline ceased operations. The letters bearing these stamps had only a short life and became rare collectors' pieces.

The period after the First World War witnessed the development of long-distance flights. In 1919 the Atlantic was successfully flown by Alcock and Brown. They and other aviators (who did not

succeed) carried mail franked by various special stamps provided by the Newfoundland Post Office and most of these are now of the greatest rarity.

The first airmail between Great Britain and Australia was transported in February 1920 by a team led by the Australian pilot, Ross Smith. The Australian authorities issued a special label which was affixed to mail flown on this occasion. These "stamps", depicting maps of England and Australia, are among the great rarities of the airpost.

In May 1920 the Italian flier, Francisco de Pinedo, succeeded in transporting mailbags from Newfoundland to Rome! A special stamp was produced for the occasion. Subsequently de Pinedo flew round the world and mail carried by him on these flights bore special postmarks of Japan and the Philippines.

Meanwhile the French were successful in establishing links between Toulouse and Morocco though airmen with engine trouble were often captured and tortured by rebel desert tribesmen and only returned after a large ransom had been paid.

During the 1920s regular air routes were gradually developed, from Toulouse to Casablanca and thence to Stanleyville (Kinshasa). British airmen pioneered the route from Cairo to Baghdad and the Near East.

Dutch aviators opened up the route to the Indies. Internal airlines operated in Canada and Australia in this period, the aircraft often flying over vast areas of underdeveloped territory. In Europe numerous national airlines linked the capital cities. Lufthansa, KLM and other world-famous companies had their tentative beginnings in this decade. In the 1930s flights became more ambitious and regular crossings of the Atlantic and the Pacific were made. This was also the period of the great polar flights. As aircraft developed in range and speed the planet Earth gradually seemed to shrink in size. The pioneer flights, both internal and world-wide, have all left their mark in the stamp album with commemorative stamps, first flight covers, postcards and other souvenirs.

THE CASUALTIES

We have already seen how Boyle's flight ended in a field. The mail carried on that occasion ranks as the first "crash mail" of a regular airline. Since then, unfortunately, there have been many other examples of this sort. Covers salvaged from air crashes have always proved a rare and particularly moving collection. Stained by immersion in sea water, or

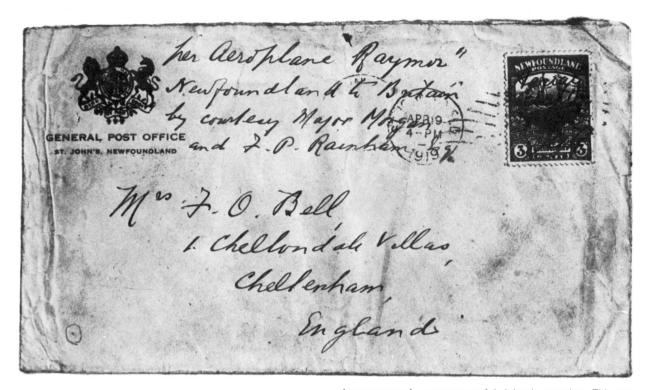

A memento of an unsuccessful Atlantic crossing. This rare cover was carried by Major Morgan and Mr. S. P. Rainham on their first attempt to fly the Atlantic, in 1919. On the eve of their departure, the Postmaster-General at St. Johns inscribed a few copies of the 3 cent caribou stamp with the words "Aerial Atlantic Mail" and added his initials. His inscription was over-optimistic, for the flight failed.

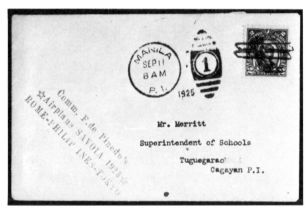

A cover flown by the Marchese de Pinedo, Manila, 1925 with a special cachet and aeroplane postmark.

A consular airmail service operated between the Russian Embassy in Berlin and Russia in the early 1920s. This cover, bearing the special Russian air stamps with values in German Marks, is addressed to Bela Kun, erstwhile head of the Hungarian communist republic of 1919. He subsequently headed the international section of the comintern in Moscow and died in the Stalinist purges of the 1930s.

charred by fire, these tragic mementoes often bear official markings indicating the circumstances of the accident, the date and even the type of aircraft involved. These items are comparatively scarce but are rich in human interest. The following examples of mail casualties are not necessarily the most rare, but are highly significant. On July 1, 1927 the *America* under the command of Richard Byrd left New York and crashed at Ver sur Mer (Calvados) in France. The mail was salvaged.

On February 19, 1929 the France–Indochina mail left Paris and was damaged in the fire which destroyed the aircraft at Moulmain in Burma. The salvaged letters completed the journey to Saigon by rail.

On June 13, 1930 the Frenchman Guillaumet had an accident right in the Cordilleras in the Andes, in the Diamanti Valley; the machine and the mail were not recovered until some months later. The non-stop France–Japan flight (on July 14, 1931) crashed at Nijni-Oudinsk. In 1929 the flight between Seville and New York had suffered the same fate.

Today, air disasters are, fortunately, less common; however, the speed and size of the planes involved make it most unlikely that any mail can be recovered from a major crash.

OTHER AIR POSTS

Several attempts have been made to carry mail by glider, but it is impossible to establish a regular service by this means. In August 1924, during a flying competition in the Rhineland in Germany, the pilot Espenlaub carried a bag of mail from Wasserkuppe to Gersfeld. In 1933 Robert Kronfield, one of the greatest gliding champions of the interwar period, flew by glider from Vienna to Semmering with the Austrian mails. In addition, the glider *Austria II* made an international flight, from Graz to Maribor (Austria–Yugoslavia); mail carried on that occasion was marked with a special cachet.

In July 1933 there was even a round trip by glider from Vienna to Vienna, via Budapest, Trieste, Milan, Zurich, Innsbruck and Salzburg! Experiments were made in the United States in 1934 using a powered aircraft to tow a string of gliders. The following year the American aviator, O'Meara, took his "sky train" to Cuba and organized a mail service between Havana and Miami. This scheme had official blessing and the Cuban postal authorities even issued a special air stamp for use on mail flown by the sky train.

In the same year, 1935, the helicopter made its debut as a mail-carrier, the inaugural flight taking

Canada was one of the foremost pioneers of internal air networks and the inauguration of each new route was marked by special covers with attractive pictorial cachets. This cover of June 1939 marks the first flight from Shediac in New Brunswick to Botwood in Newfoundland.

Cover from Naples to RAF Hinaidi, Mesopotamia, September 1926. Note the airmail postmarks of Brindisi, which was an important staging post on pre-war international air routes — just as, a century earlier, it had been an important port of call for international shipping. Below: the additional stamps on the back of the envelope have also been cancelled with Brindisi airmail postmarks.

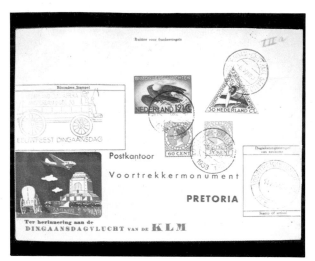

The close ties between the Soviet Union and the German Weimar republic are reflected in this pictorial airmail postmark of 1929, applied to mail flown between Leningrad and Berlin.

An airmail cover of February 1925, bearing the complete Syrian air series of 1924 – French stamps overprinted by the Capuchin Fathers of Beirut. Note the endorsement indicating the route via Baghdad to Cairo.

A round-flight cover celebrating the South African national holiday, Dingaansday. The cover, franked with Dutch Special Flight stamps, left Amsterdam on 6 December 1938 and was postmarked at the Voortrekker (Pioneer) Monument, Pretoria on 14 December. It was then mailed back to Holland, franked with a pair of the Voortrekker stamps and arrived at Amsterdam on 7 January 1939.

A cover flown from England to Australia in 1919–20 by the Australian team led by Ross and Keith Smith. A special stamp was affixed to all mail on arrival in Australia, to celebrate the occasion.

Below: An American airport dedication cover. Like Canada, the United States developed an intricate network of internal air routes in the 1920s. The inauguration of new airports was marked by souvenir covers and cachets.

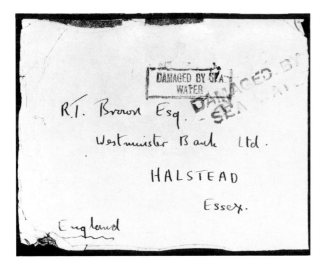

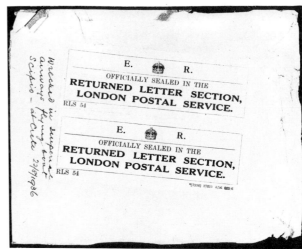

A cover salvaged from the crash of the Imperial Airways flying boat *Scipio* at Crete, on 22 August 1936. Note the explanatory cachets ''Damaged by sea water'' and (right) the official seals of the Returned Letter Section of the London post office.

Gerhard Zucker, the German rocket pioneer, was responsible for several important mail-carrying rocket flights in the 1930s. This cover was carried by a rocket launched in the Netherlands in 1935. Zucker subsequently worked on the V-1 and V-2 rocket projects.

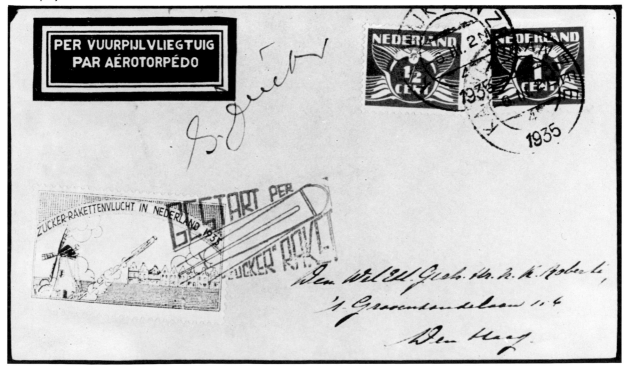

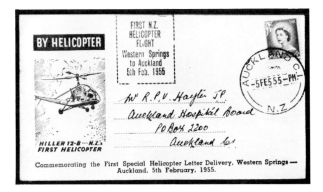

As part of the celebrations marking the Brussels World Fair and the Belgica Philatelic Exhibitions of 1935, covers were flown by an experimental rocket between Duinbergen and Heyst. Special labels, postmarks and cachets were provided for this event.

Above, left: A contrast of old and new methods of mail communications is provided by this picture of mail being transferred from a helicopter to a deer sledge in the Evenk National Park of the Soviet Union.

Cover flown by Hiller 12-B helicopter on the first New Zealand helicopter flight, February 1955, from Western Springs to Auckland. Helicopters have been used increasingly since the end of World War II for short-haul airmail flights in the United States, Britain and many European countries.

place on May 25 between Camden (New Jersey) and the offices of the Greyhound Corporation.

In 1933 a radio-controlled pilotless plane had been used to carry mail from Los Angeles to New York. The letters were said to bear (for we have never seen any!) the cachet "Carried on first Robot controlled plane non-stop flight leaving Los Angeles Municipal Airport 5.51 a.m. June 2, 1933, arriving Floyd Bennet Air Port 10.19 p.m. June 2, 1933". Here, perhaps, is the future.

Remaining in the sky, we must conclude with postal services by parachute. Various devices have been invented for the purpose. Free fall parachutes are the type most commonly used, but other kinds have been used in which the canister falls swiftly and the chute opens only as the canister nears the ground, giving the mailbags a soft landing. Parachute mail, complete with special postmarks and cachets, has been recorded from France, Hungary, Thailand, Britain and the United States. In the Postal Museum

in Berne, Switzerland, you can see the padded containers, with long red and white streamers attached, which were used by the Zeppelins to jettison mail while in flight.

Experiments have been made since the late 1920s in the carriage of mail by rocket, but this method has not yet been exploited commercially. In 1969 the Apollo XI crew took a letter with them to the moon and there they franked it with a stamp which they actually printed on the lunar ground. The steel die used for the moon stamp was subsequently brought back to earth and used in the production of a 10 cent stamp depicting the first men on the moon, but available for more mundane postage!

Without doubt the posts have conquered the air, for much of the development in aerial transportation has only been possible as a result of generous aid and subsidies from postal administrations. Future generations may witness interplanetary mail and accept it as a commonplace.

A memento of the epic siege of Leningrad during World War II.
This much-redirected item bears a Soviet field post office
mark (No. 521) and the Leningrad date-stamp of 17 May 1942.

6

The post in wartime

WE HAVE SEEN how the postal services of the world evolved over the centuries, adapting themselves gradually to new techniques, and overcoming the problems of distance, difficult terrain and climates. Too often, however, wars have broken out between nations, paralyzing communications and setting the postal authorities a whole new set of problems. As usual they took up the challenge, and some of their ingenious solutions are described here.

Everyone knows the story of the famous soldier from Marathon who in 490 B.C. fell dead after bringing word of the victory. He might be considered the forefather of military despatch riders. Nearer the present day, illuminated manuscripts in the Middle ages, like the ones in the Chronicle of Drebold Schilling, show how messengers from the battlefield were given special protection, and were distinguished by their uniform. Methods have changed a great deal since then, but communications are still of paramount importance in wartime.

TRANSMISSION OF MILITARY ORDERS

Before the present era of ultra-rapid communications by tele-printer and telecommunications satellite, armies in the field had grave problems of communication. It was very difficult for staff officers to have an up-to-date assessment of the situation so as to give detailed orders to troop formations. Naturally secrecy was also an important factor. Use was made of highly skilled horsemen and relays were used over longer distances, in the same manner as the civil posts of that time. Speed was the watchword, but various ingenious devices were used to conceal the despatches – the hollow knob of a cane, hollow coins which unscrewed to reveal the message inside, the hollow sole of a boot, and so forth. Others committed the message to memory and carried nothing.

The Emperor Napoleon set up a perfect system. The despatches were locked in a special portfolio to which only the emperor and his correspondents held a key. This portfolio was accompanied by a small

Right: Claude Chappe (1763–1805) invented an optical telegraph system in 1791. In 1794, it was adopted by the French army, and a chain of 16 relay-stations was set up, linking Paris with Lille. Later, Paris was linked to all the frontiers.
Below, right: The telegraph post at Montmartre.

The envoy of Count Valangin brings a declaration of war to the citizens of Berne in 1339 (from the Chronicle of Drebold Schilling).

book. Both were carried at full speed from post to post, the times of arrival and departure being written in at each halt. Any courier who was late was imprisoned for 24 hours, and if he were late twice was dismissed from service. Every day, a portfolio left Paris for Naples, Milan, Madrid, Lisbon, Tilsit, Vienna, Bratislava and Amsterdam. The relay system was so efficient that Napoleon received news in eight days from Milan and in fifteen from Naples.

For the journey between Naples and Alexandria the Emperor allowed 100 hours maximum. For ordinary communications he established a system of 20 mail-coaches which ran, ten per day, day and night between the major towns. Napoleon also moved whole regiments by mail-coach. This must have been a major undertaking as the horses had to be changed every hour.

Another famous example, though on a different level, is that of the scouts in the Boer War. In 1899 and 1900, Mafeking was besieged. The town was about five miles in circumference and Lord Cecil, Chief of Staff, had only 700 soldiers and 300 civilians to defend it. The remaining population was 600 white women and children and 7,000 natives. This was the total strength of his force. Baden-Powell, the founder of the Boy Scout movement, organized a corp of cadets to undertake liaison work. They even managed to set up a local postal service between the town and the forts, with special postage stamps depicting a cadet with a haversack, on a bicycle.

MILITARY TELEGRAPHS

An indispensable method of communicating in wartime is the telegraph, which was modernised from the end of the eighteenth century. The credit for reviving the idea of visual communication, goes to the French engineer, Claude Chappe, who in 1791 invented an ingenious optical telegraph system. He made several attempts to establish communications by this method, but the people destroyed his apparatus and accused him of espionage. Nothing daunted, he continued his experiments and in 1793 he gave an official demonstration over a distance of 20 miles. Shortly afterwards, the Convention decided to set up a telegraph line between Paris and Lille where French troops were fighting Austrian forces. In 1794 towers equipped with signalling apparatus were placed at regular intervals along the route, there being sixteen of them in a distance of 140 miles. With these military despatches could be transmitted to Paris in a matter of minutes. The men transmitting the messages could not decipher them, for a form of shorthand was used, with groups of

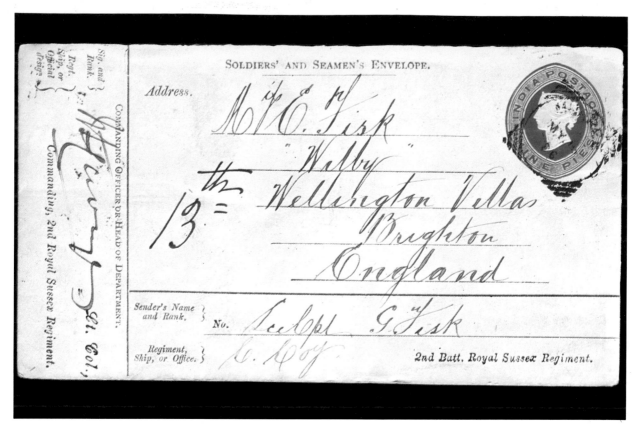

Soldiers' and Seamen's Envelope.

After the introduction of adhesive stamps, special stamped envelopes and postcards were provided for the use of soldiers and seamen. The cover had to be endorsed by the commanding officer of the unit in which the sender was serving.

A much-travelled cover from the period of the Russo-Turkish War for the liberation of Bulgaria. It bears the transit postmarks of Ungeny, Rushchuk, Sofia, Ikhtiman, Sliven, Plovdiv, Pazardzhik and back through Sofia and Ungeny to Odessa: the post office failed to locate the addressee.

numerals substituted for words and even whole phrases. A whole phrase would be represented by two figures. In time, Paris was linked to all the frontiers and with the advance of the French armies the military telegraph system was extended into Belgium, Holland, Italy and Germany where it rendered invaluable service.

In 1834 a telegraph line was opened between St. Petersburg and Kronstadt, with five stations in between. In March 1838 St. Petersburg was linked to Warsaw by 148 stations, each of which was manned by a staff of four. In his enthusiasm, Tsar Nicholas I granted a pension of 10,000 roubles and the Order of St. Vladimir to the French engineer, P. J. Chatau, who installed this line.

In Prussia, Karl Pistor installed a telegraph system between Berlin and Coblenz.

A mobile optical system operated by a specially trained corps was attached to the French armies during the conquest of Algeria in 1830. This telegraph corps also served during the Crimean War in 1855. A despatch of 25 words could be sent in 15 minutes from the general headquarters to the army corps; in 25 minutes to the Baidar Valley; and in 30 minutes to Egry-Adgadj. For the same distances a despatch rider on horseback would need from thirty

minutes to four hours and ran the risk of being shot.

Bit by bit the electric telegraph replaced the old optical system. It was first used militarily during the American Civil War. At the commencement of hostilities the Federal Army had two distinct corps, one purely military, which had existed before the campaign and known as the "meteorological corps"; and the other a corps composed entirely of telegraphists. In the course of operations, and after two years campaigning, the military corps was disbanded on November 10, 1863, and the officers, men and equipment transferred to the civil service.

The decision of the War Minister was based on the fact that "although the organization is a military one, it was not as good as the corps of civilians who were well trained in their telegraphing." A report from Colonel Stager to General Meigs described the role of the telegraphists:

"All round the camps the vigilance of the telegraphists could be felt at all times. Close by the sentinels, at every hour of day or night, one could make out the sounds of their equipment. In the heat of battle, amid the bullets, the unarmed telegraphists moved like silent and invisible shadows."

During the four years of the Civil War, over 15,000 miles of telegraph line were laid, many of them under

Right: Cover from Danville, Virginia, used locally during the American Civil War. Note the elaborate stamp printed on the top left-hand corner of the cover. Many postmasters in the Southern Confederacy produced their own stamps and postal stationery in 1861, before the general series of the Confederate States became available.

Far right: The Pacific War of 1879–81 between Chile, Peru and Bolivia produced many interesting items of postal history. This cover of April 1881 bears the markings of the Posts of the Army in the Field, in conjunction with the Valparaiso Franca stamp.

Below, right: Although postal rates in the nineteenth century were generally high, soldiers and sailors on active service enjoyed preferential treatment. Letters from soldiers serving in India were charged threepence to the recipient in England, and special marks indicating the charge were applied at various points on entry to the United Kingdom. This letter of 1828, from a soldier in India, bears the Calcutta Ship Letter mark and the Portsmouth "India Soldiers" mark.

Rushing to post a letter during the Franco-Prussian War: German troops handing letters to a horseman of the Field Post.

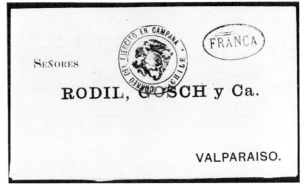

enemy fire; 25 telegraphists were killed, 71 were made prisoner and many more were seriously wounded. Their equipment cost $2,655,500 and the number of telegrams transmitted ran to over 6,500,000.

The Prussian troops in the war of 1870–71 used telegraphic equipment while campaigning in France. Under the direction of Colonel Meydam a total of 6,770 miles of line were laid.

During the First World War telegraphs became increasingly important. By this time there had been great progress, and actual live conversations were possible. Wireless telegraphy began to be developed only at the end of that war. Finally in the 1939–45 war, thanks to enormous advances in technique, radio played a large part on all fronts, and was used by both sides; with teleprinters, radio has been an indispensable feature of more localized conflicts since then.

SOLDIERS' MAIL

The mobilization of millions of men inevitably poses enormous problems to the postal services of all countries. Moreover the need for troops on active service to communicate regularly and promptly with their families is recognized as an important factor in the maintenance of morale.

International co-operation is evident in this Boxer Rebellion postcard, bearing stamps of the German and Indian contingents, cancelled at their respective field post offices.

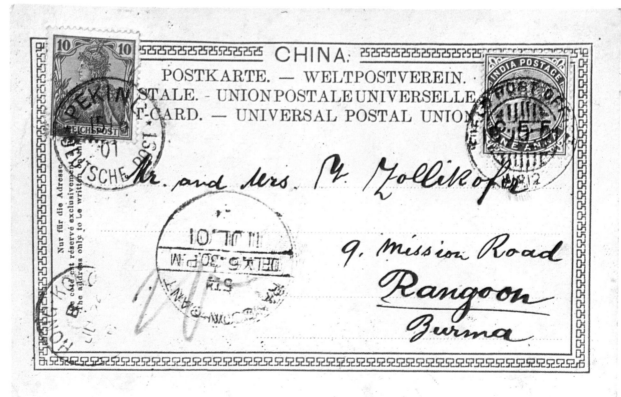

The Chinese Boxer Rebellion of 1900 led to international
intervention. The stamps and covers of twelve different nations
were used in this campaign. This cover bears Indian stamps
overprinted C.E.F. (Chinese Expeditionary Force), cancelled by
C.E.F. Field Post Office No. 1.

A relic of the ill-fated Russo-Japanese War of 1905–6 is this
patriotic postcard, postmarked at Yokohama in March 1906.
Cards such as this were sold on behalf of the Red Cross and
war charity funds.

The Balkan Wars which formed the prelude to World War I also produced a fine crop of military postal souvenirs. This Salonika cover bears a Red Cross charity stamp provided by the Greek authorities.

Right: A cover from Cuba to Spain during the rebellion of 1896–7, bearing the military cachet of an artillery unit operating against the Cuban rebels.

Some of the postmarks used during the Anglo-Boer War of 1899–1902 were unusually large and colourful. This British postcard was sent from Volksrust in November 1900 to Tuticorin in India. Ordinary British stamps and stationery were used by troops on active service in South Africa.

A YMCA cover franked by a British 1½ penny stamp during World War I. Note the mute cancellation, employed at many British sea ports to conceal the movement of shipping and naval units, and also the censor mark of the United States Naval Forces.

The German postal service during the First World War carried, it is said, the record number of 17 thousand millions of items of correspondence to German soldiers who in turn sent 11 thousand millions of letters back to their families. When one considers that that country put 242 divisions into the field these statistics become more credible. In the same war, the French military postal system handled on average $3\frac{1}{2}$ million letters a day and 200,000 parcels. In 1918 the yearly total rose to 4 thousand million letters and 75 million parcels.

Apart from the numbers involved, the mobility of troops presents a great problem, while the need to preserve a measure of secrecy about troop movement and the size of the army further complicates the handling of mail. In 1914 France inaugurated a system of centralizing all forces' mail; letters were then distributed to military units in the field. Each sector had a postal sector number, so that a division could be reached no matter where it was fighting.

The British army serving on the Western Front had a mail train operating a shuttle service from Boulogne to Cologne in 1919. A staff of four men of the Royal Engineers manned the sorting carriage. There were six trains, called the *Adriatic*, *Arctic*, *Atlantic*, *Baltic*, *Oceanic* and *Pacific*. Servicemen were allowed to post letters and cards in any train's letter box. The heating and lighting in the postal trains were provided by petrol or acetylene but after a terrible explosion which killed the postal workers, electricity was installed in the wagons.

Special postmarks with A.P.O. (Army Post Office) or F.P.O. (Field Post Office) were used by the British military postal service, with a distinguishing number, and this system has continued in use to the present day. A similar system has been adopted by the fieldposts of other countries. In 1939–45 the German *Feldpost* worked like this: the National Post (*Reichspost*) collected together all the military mail and sent it to the *Feldpost* who checked and distributed it.

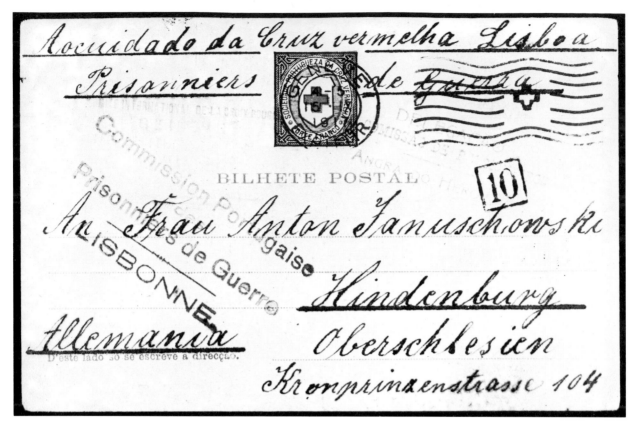

The good offices of Portugal, neutral in both world wars, were used to maintain contact with prisoners-of-war. This card, produced by the Portuguese Red Cross, concerns a prisoner-of-war in Upper Silesia, during World War I.

Above, right: A registered cover from Legionowo in Nazi-occupied Poland, bearing the label and postal marking of the German Field Post.

Below, right: Patriotic covers, embellished with the Stars and Stripes, have been popular in the United States since the Civil War. This cover, on behalf of the United States Navy, dates from 1918. Personnel on active service did not have to add stamps to their mail.

Obviously, the same system worked in reverse. A code number from a secret list was given in place of an address and the route taken by a letter varied according to where the fighting was taking place.

Some cases were very complicated and necessitated the collaboration of several countries. For example the mail for French forces under General de Gaulle (who were stationed in North Africa) was sent via North America in 1943–44. Several French ships had spent some time being refitted and armed in the U.S.A. before going on to Africa and close links were maintained between the United States and French sailors. The chief of the American military postal service authorised the transmission of French mail by the U.S. Air Force at the average rate of 6 cents the half ounce. American airmail stamps were sold by post orderlies and French shipping offices. They were franked by the Fleet Mail Office. Subsequently these stamps were overprinted RF (*République Française*) and examples of these letters are now highly prized.

PRISONER-OF-WAR MAIL

Inevitably in wartime servicemen get captured by the enemy and are put in prisoner-of-war camps. For months – or even years – they have had to wait there. For humanitarian reasons they are usually allowed to correspond briefly with their families, though mail is censored. During the Napoleonic wars arrangements were made for French prisoners to write to their families from the prison ships where they were held. Special letter sheets were provided and even distinctive oval postmarks used, all of which are very rare today.

It is in Europe that the greatest variety of correspondence can be found. Special facilities were provided through the International Red Cross for French troops interned in Switzerland during and after the Franco-Prussian War of 1870–71 and a similar system was resurrected in the First World War by the same society, whose delegates visited the prison camps. The Red Cross produced a series of picture

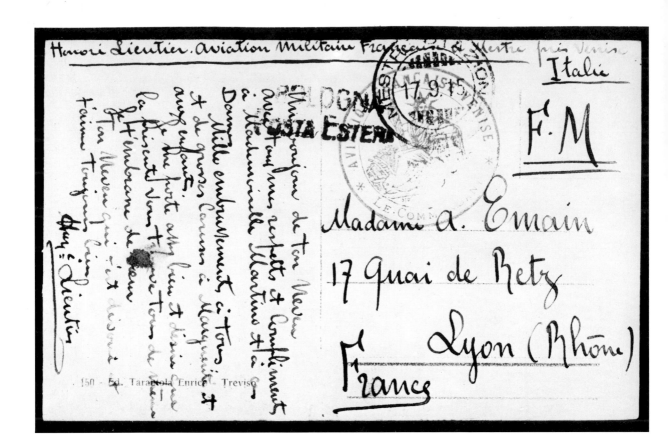

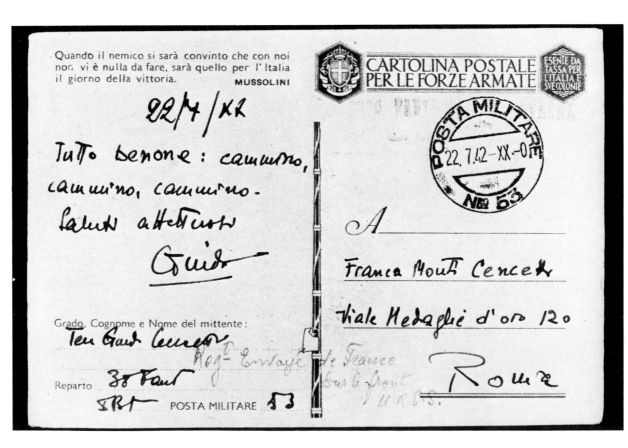

The liberation of France in World War II is reflected in this cover of November 1944, bearing French stamps cancelled at an American Army Post Office. This letter, written by H. K. Robinson, was apparently censored by him, too.

Above, left: A postcard despatched from a French military aviation unit stationed in Italy during World War I. Note the "Bologna Posta Estero" cachet, applied at Bologna to mail going abroad.

Left: An Italian military franking of 1942. Special postcards were issued to the armed forces to send messages home from the front. The cards served a dual purpose: the picture was often a propaganda instrument.

postcards illustrating the various camps and a collection of these is of exceptional documentary interest. The cards featured general views of the camps, the prisoners' work, recreation, crafts (tailoring, cooking etc.) roll-call, the hospitals and even the camp cemeteries. Altogether the different cards numbered 78 (Germany), Britain and colonies (39), Austria-Hungary (27), France and North Africa (128), Italy (20), Japan (12), Russia (17) and Turkey (12).

During the Second World War the Germans succeeded in capturing millions of enemy troops, as did the Russians. Some idea of the complex system of camps and their postal arrangements may be gained from the breakdown of the French camps in Germany. Private soldiers and NCOs were held in 72 *Stalags* numbered from 1 to 21, the numbers being followed by letters such as 13a (Bad Sulzbach), 13b (Weiden), 13c (Hamelburg), 13d (Nürnberg Langwasser). Officers were held in the *Oflags*, numbering 47 in all. French colonial troops – Algerians, Moroccans, Senegalese and Annamites were held in *Front-Stalags*. Finally there were various "reprisal camps", all situated in Poland, where prisoners who had refused to work or had attempted to escape, were held.

Families could write only on the reply half of the cards sent to them by each prisoner. These cards were

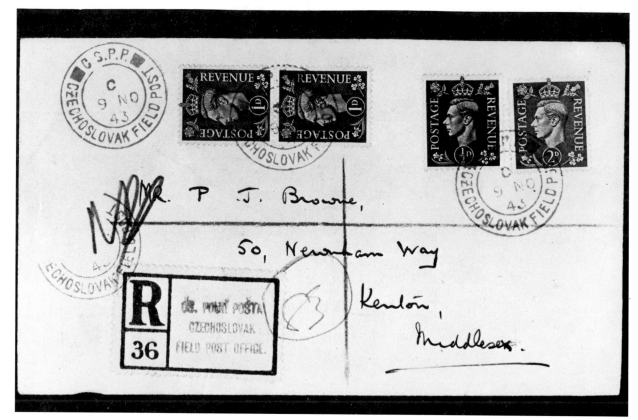

Troops from countries overrun by Germany in World War II found a refuge in Britain, where they regrouped and later took part in the liberation of Europe. This registered cover of November 1943 bears British stamps, cancelled by the field postmark of the Czechoslovak forces.

Above, right: Patriotic items in pre-revolutionary Russia portrayed popular heroes. This colourful postcard shows the Grand Duke Alexei, uncle of the Tsar and Commander of the armies in the field at the beginning of World War I.

Below, right: A memento of the Six Day War of June, 1967 – an Arab enquiry about a missing soldier, written on an official Red Cross letter form.

headed *Kriegsgefangenenpost* (Prisoner-of-War Post) and gave detailed instructions, in German, for use, as well as containing spaces for the prisoner's number, rank and name, his camp number and its location. Only seven lines were reserved for the actual communication, and for the prisoner's news a similar space was allotted. A few very rare examples exist, with 19 lines for the message.

Some soldiers fled to Switzerland where they were housed in camps. In June 1940 more than 30,000 French went to Switzerland. They were distributed to 200 centres, but following an agreement with the Germans they were set free in 1941. The same thing had happened in 1914 and in 1870 when General Bourbaki's army was forced to cross the frontier.

In this neutral country many private committees helped the Red Cross to comfort the prisoners of war on both sides and special stationery for the use of

prisoners has been recorded in both world wars with the cachets of the British, French, German, Belgian, Italian and Russian Red Cross, as well as the various civic bodies in Switzerland.

CIVILIAN INTERNEES

Modern total warfare is not content to inflict hardship on the combatants. It has resulted in the deportation and internment of civilians – men, women and children – on the pretext of race or nationality. The human herds which were a reproach to antiquity (such as the Babylonian captivity of the Jews) have had their modern counterpart in the uprooting, herding together and maltreatment of innocent people in the course of the last world war, not to mention subsequent upheavals in Biafra, Bangladesh and Vietnam.

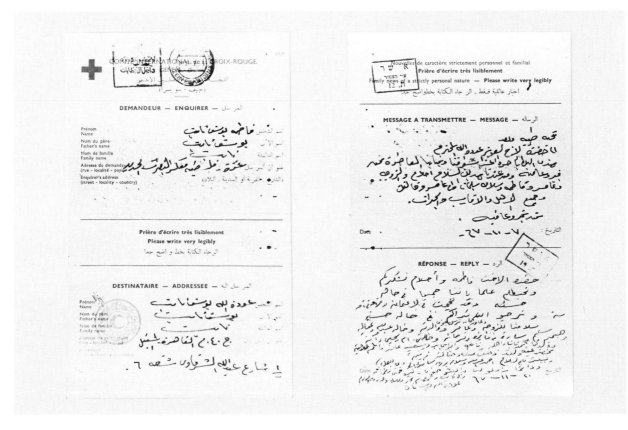

Civilian internees enjoyed much the same mail facilities as prisoners-of-war. This envelope, from an internee in neutral Denmark in May 1916, bears the cachet of the garrison headquarters in Aarhus.

Above, left: The Suez expedition of 1956 is recalled by this French naval cover of October 1956, with the cachets of the *Marcel le Bihan* aircraft carrier and "Service de la Mer".

Left: Special envelopes and postcards were used for prisoners-of-war mail during both world wars. This card, from the German camp at Soltau, is addressed to Liège, Belgium, March 1916.

The most notorious examples of this human displacement were provided by the Nazi concentration camps and those infamous places have their place in postal history. In Alsace, for example, was the Vorbrück Concentration camp, served by the post office at Schirmeck. On the pathetic cards sent by deportees to their families the philatelist may read the printed publicity notices vaunting the charms of the region and its attractions as a winter sports centre. The camp at Natzweiler, also known as Struthof, preserves to this day a sinister reputation for cruelty.

There are numerous postal markings from these dreadful places. Cards with such postmarks as *Mauthausen/Gusen*; *Konzentrationlager Auschwitz, Postzensurstelle K-Z Dachau Geprüft* (passed by the postal censor at Dachau), *SS Feldpost/Waffen, SS/Aigle/ Dienststempel/SS, Totenkopfstrurmbann, Buchenwald* or *Gross Rosen* – the so-called camp for intellectuals.

There were other types of camp for civilians who collaborated with the Germans, others in neutral countries for civilians from the countries at war, and yet others in the countries at war for their own national enemies. In all these cases the post continued to function in some way, providing the only tenuous link with the outside world and normality.

The turbulent period since the end of the Second

Boer prisoners taken during the South African war were sent to camps in St. Helena. This cover of 1900 shows an Orange Free State stamp overprinted by the British occupation forces and the prisoner-of-war censor mark, addressed to a Boer prisoner at Greenpoint, St. Helena.

An internee's letter from Germany, January 1941, bearing camp cachets and the German "Geprüft" (censored) mark, addressed to Geneva in neutral Switzerland.

A postcard from the Warsaw Ghetto, October 1941. It bears the cachet of the Jewish Council (*Judenrat*), and German military censor marks, and is addressed to neutral Switzerland.

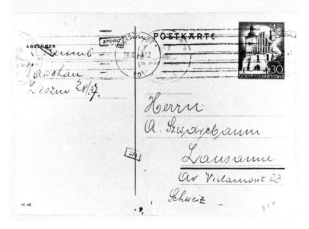

World War has witnessed many minor conflicts as well as the so-called Cold War, which stops just short of actual hostilities. This period is reflected in the postal arrangements for communication between the two halves of such divided countries as Germany, Vietnam and Korea. The upheavals in Berlin during the blockade, the Hungarian uprising and the Czech invasion of 1968 all have their record in stamps, postmarks and postal history.

CLANDESTINE POSTS

In occupied countries, patriots keep up their resistance and must have very secret methods of communicating and of intercepting the enemy's mail. Let us take the example of the postwoman Juliette Dodu, who was 20 when the Prussians invaded France in 1870. She tapped the German telegraph wires and intercepted messages passing between Prince Frederick Charles and his Chief of Staff. She passed on this intelligence to the French authorities and was the means of saving many French soldiers' lives. She was denounced to the Germans by a domestic servant, tried by court martial and condemned to death. Prince Frederick pardoned her and congratulated her on her bravery.

Right: A poignant reminder of the heroic Warsaw Rising of September 1944, this letter bears the fleur-de-lis postmark of the Polish Boy Scouts, who operated the mail service during the rising. Above are examples of the different postmarks that were used.

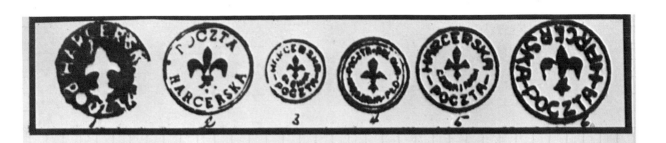

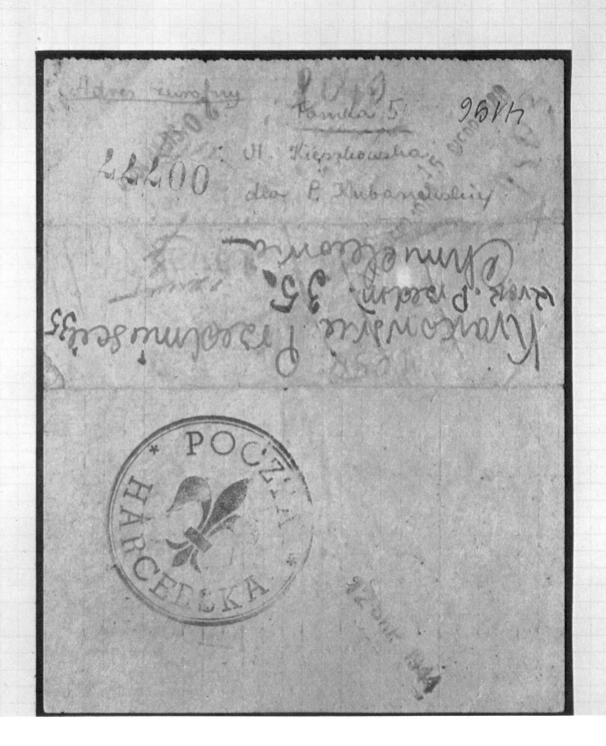

After the German invasion of Russia in 1941, a large part of Transnistria and Bukovina was ceded to Rumania. This card bears the Rumanian postmark of Odesa (Odessa) and the censor mark of Chisinau. Note the special Transnistrian stamps, issued by Rumania to celebrate the annexation.

Right: A cover from the Dutch Indies internment camp at Medan addressed to the International Red Cross in Geneva. Note the British and Dutch censor marks and the internment camp postmark.

Some 72 years later the French resistance pulled off an identical but very important coup. The patriotic postmen built telephone equipment similar to that used by the Germans. They caused very short but realistic breakdowns in transmission, which gave them time to intercept long-distance cables from German headquarters between Paris – Metz and Paris – Strasbourg, going to Germany. The conversations they intercepted were reported to Allied intelligence.

Underground postal service operated in Poland in the same period, and even used stamps which were similar in design to those used by the Polish government exiled in Britain. A more recent example was the clandestine post organized by the rebels in Algeria in 1959–60, before the country gained independence. The *fellaqahs* were organized into *merquez* or semi-fixed postal stations which moved continually within a small radius. The *Katibas* or combat forces were groups of 100–200 well-armed men who kept hidden in the bush. Communication between headquarters and the *katibas* was kept up by the *merquez*. Every night, *tissals* (guides) operated in relays to carry messages from one *merquez* to another, following a recommended route. Mail was inserted in very small envelopes bearing a seal and stuck down with sticky

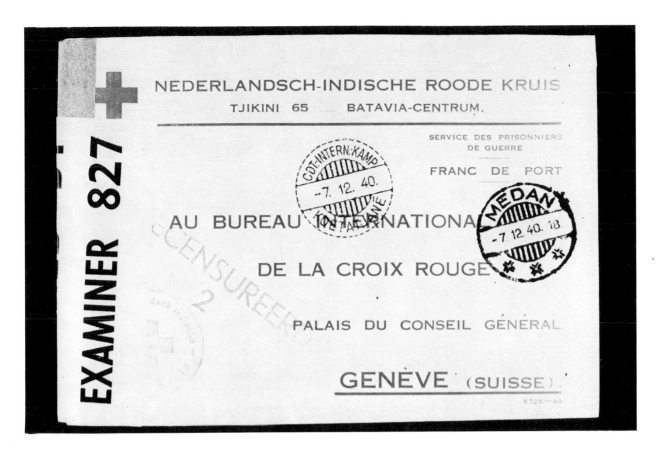

NEDERLANDSCH-INDISCHE ROODE KRUIS

TJIKINI 65   BATAVIA-CENTRUM.

SERVICE DES PRISONNIERS
DE GUERRE

FRANC DE PORT

AU BUREAU INTERNATIONAL

DE LA CROIX ROUGE

PALAIS DU CONSEIL GÉNÉRAL

GENÈVE (SUISSE)

tape. The well-planned routes along which the mail moved followed the river edges of two French military sectors. The fellaqahs who carried it knew that the French always kept well within these boundaries to be on the safe side. Only military or political mail was carried secretly like this, and the soldiers doing the work had usually no way of corresponding with their families and friends. On arrival, the letters had to be destroyed and the only ones known to exist today come from mail intercepted by the French and kept unlawfully as a souvenir by the soldiers.

CENSORED MAIL

As a security measure governments in wartime impose strict control over correspondence, as well as over printed matter and newspapers. Official censorship in one form or another has been used for a very long time but the majority of examples relate to the two world wars and the lesser campaigns of the present century. Letters were officially opened, read by censors and then resealed. Anything considered militarily dangerous or bad for morale was made illegible. A fine collection of censor markings and official seals from many countries could be formed.

Napoleon I ordered all mail coming from Britain to be stopped and imposed a total embargo on letters from that source. The English opened letters written by their prisoners of war and stamped them with a crown and the words "Transport Official Prisoners of War". Even earlier, the Jacobite rebellion of 1745–6 provides one of the oldest records of censorship. Letters from Edinburgh to London were intercepted by the Highlanders following Bonnie Prince Charlie, examined and then forwarded to their destination with the manuscript endorsement "Opened by the Rebels". During the war of 1812–14 between Britain and the United States an oval censor mark inscribed "Examined Marshal's Office Massachusetts", with a radiating eye in the centre was used on mail emanating from Boston. During the American War of Independence mail was opened by both sides and marked "Prisoner's letter examined".

The Boer War of 1899–1902 provides a vast number of examples of censor markings from all over South Africa, on both the Boer and the British sides. Incidentally, many of these censor markings were used on mail from Boer prisoners interned in Bermuda and St. Helena.

During the First World War mail from prisoners captured by the Allies in the Dardanelles campaign was censored in Egypt or Malta, where the prisoners

Right: A Red Cross postcard with Italian and Austrian prisoner-of-war censor marks, from Austria to Italy and redirected to Spezia, July 1916.

Below, right: Although the Netherlands was under German occupation, the Dutch colony of Curaçao carried on the struggle for national survival. This cover bears a cachet celebrating "Princess Juliana in our Midst", as well as the "Gezien" (censored) mark of St. Maarten.

Croatia was established as a fascist puppet state, after the Axis invasion of Yugoslavia in 1941. This express, registered airmail cover from Zagreb to Germany bears the stamp and special postmark celebrating the third anniversary of the Croat Labour Front.

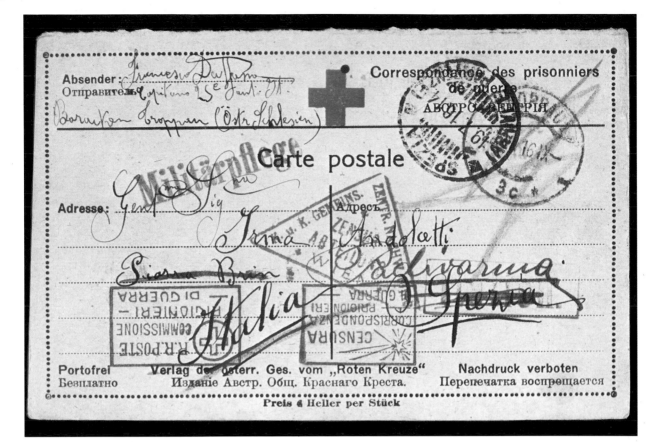

were held and covers may be found with the initials PC or PBC (Passed By Censor). The Spanish Civil War and the Second World War continued the tradition of censorship on both sides. Mail from Britain to Germany, for example, passed through neutral Switzerland or Portugal, and covers may be found with both British and Nazi censor marks. The Germans eventually devised a complicated system of code letters to indicate the origin and destination of letters passing from one part of occupied territory to another or going to neutral countries. The main censor offices were located in Koenigsberg (for the Baltic and USSR), Berlin (airmail to the United States and Latin America), Cologne (northern France and the Low Countries), Munich (Italy, Spain and Portugal), Frankfurt (Switzerland, southern France and the United States), Hamburg (the Scandinavian countries), and Vienna (the Balkan countries).

WAR STAMPS

Special stamps produced in wartime fall into several distinct categories. The first consists of special issues made by the invading forces for use in the territory which they occupy. The earliest example of this was the series of stamps produced in 1870 for use

At the time of the German occupation of Northern France, following the British withdrawal from Dunkirk, French stamps were overprinted by the Germans to signify "Occupied District Northern France".

in occupied France. The stamps simply bore the numeral of value and the words *Postes* and *Centimes*. The progress of the German forces in both world wars is well illustrated by the stamps issued in occupied areas, consisting either of contemporary German stamps overprinted with the name or currency of the territory concerned, or of the stamps of the country overprinted to signify German occupation. The British practice, on the other hand, was to overprint the stamps of the enemy territory with the royal monogram: V.R.I. or E.R.I. on stamps of the Transvaal and the Orange Free State during the Boer War and G.R.I. on stamps of the German colonies in the First World War. Indian stamps were overprinted C.E.F. (Chinese Expeditionary Force) during the Boxer Rebellion of 1900, I.E.F. (Indian Expeditionary Force) for use in Mesopotamia and the Western Front in the First World War. In civil wars, such as the Spanish one in 1936–39, both sides printed stamps with different designs.

Another category of war stamp includes those issued to raise funds for war charity or as a tax on correspondence to help the war effort. The Spanish civil wars of the nineteenth century, and the Spanish American War of 1898–99 resulted in the issue of stamps inscribed *Impuesto da Guerra* (War Tax). Many

Numerous stamps, charity labels and items of postal stationery were produced by the protagonists in the Spanish Civil War of 1936–39. This postcard was issued on behalf of the Red International and bears a local stamp issued by the republicans in the Asturias.

Top: White Russian refugees, led by General Baron von Wrangel, were evacuated from the Crimea in 1920 and taken to Turkey. Russian and Ukrainian stamps with a special overprint were used by the Russian Refugee Post in Turkey. This postcard bears the Russian camp postmarks of Constantinople and other internment centres.

The Yugoslav government in exile issued its own stamps in Britain during World War II. This set marked the twenty-fifth anniversary of Yugoslavia. The large, rectangular postmark indicates that this cover was posted aboard a Yugoslav ship serving with the allied navies.

Die Feldpost

Nr. 4.   8. November 1915.

Zur Kriegslage.

(Vom 17. Oktober bis zum 7. November 1915.)

Westlicher Kriegsschauplatz.

In den letzten drei Wochen hat der deutsche Generalstab eine Unmenge Soldaten hingeopfert in der Absicht, das neulich im Artois und in der Champagne verlorene Gelände zurückzuerobern. Nur eins ist ihm gelungen, nämlich die Zahl der deutschen Verluste noch zu vergrößern. In den letzten großen Schlachten haben die Deutschen an Toten, Schwerverwundeten und Gefangenen 140,000 Mann, d. h. mehrere Armeekorps, eingebüßt. Dessenungeachtet beschlossen sie die verlorenen Stellungen, wenn nicht ganz, so doch teilweise, wieder an sich zu reißen. Abgesehen von zahlreichen Lokalversuchen, führten sie folgende Massenangriffe aus:

1. Bei Givenchy versuchten sie zu 8 verschiedenen Malen, binnen 5 Tagen (zwischen dem 19. und dem 24. Oktober) die französischen Stellungen zu erstürmen; alle Anläufe brachen unter schweren Verlusten zusammen.

2. Am 19. Oktober griffen sie nach stundenlanger Artillerievorbereitung die Stellungen östlich von Rheims, auf einer Front von 10 Klm. an; sie gelangten stellenweise bis in die feindlichen Gräben, wurden aber schon am folgenden Tage durch Gegenangriffe wieder hinausgeworfen.

3. Am 21. Oktober führten sie im nämlichen Gebiete einen neuen Angriff aus, der gleich dem ersteren blutig abgewiesen wurde; die deutschen Sturmtruppen vermochten nicht einmal bis an die Drahtnetze vor den französischen Gräben heranzukommen.

Dagegen gelang es den Franzosen, sich am 25. Oktober, in der Champagne, etwa 2 Klm. nördlich von Mesnil-les-Hurlus, eines sehr wichtigen Schanzwerkes zu bemächtigen, das an Breite 1200 Meter und an Tiefe durchschnittlich 250 Meter betrug. Alle Gegenangriffe blieben erfolglos. Doch konnten die Deutschen am 31. Oktober, infolge eines blutigen Vorstoßes, auf der Höhe nördlich des Dorfes Tahure, wieder Fuß fassen; dort blieben sie aber einem fürchterlichen Artilleriefeuer ausgesetzt und waren nicht imstande, weiter vorzudringen. Auf der übrigen Front endete der ganze Angriff mit der Flucht der Sturmtruppen in den Ausgangsstellungen. Tausende von deutschen Leichen bedeckten den Boden zwischen den französischen und den deutschen Linien.

Angesichts der fortgesetzten Mißerfolge seiner Armeen auf dem westlichen Kriegsschauplatz, hat sich das deutsche Oberkommando entschlossen, eine gewisse Anzahl von Divisionen, die bis jetzt auf der russischen Front verwendet worden waren, nach Frankreich zu versetzen. Diese Truppen werden aber schwerlich ausreichen, die Lücken auszufüllen, die in den deutschen Reihen durch die französischen Geschütze verursacht worden sind. Dabei muß bemerkt werden, daß das deutsche Reich, das schon über 3 Millionen Mann verloren hat, nicht mehr imstande ist, frische Truppen nach Osten zu senden. So steht den täglich stärker werdenden Russen ein Feind gegenüber, der mit jedem Tage schwächer wird.

In Deutschland greift offensichtlich eine gewisse Mißstimmung über die Kriegslage im Westen um sich. Die Bierbank-Krieger und Maulhelden, die tagtäglich in der gemütlichen Stammkneipe hinter dem Bierkrug alle militärischen und politischen Fragen ins Reine bringen, stehen nicht an, die eigenen Truppen zu tadeln oder gar zu verspotten, die weder Paris noch Calais einzunehmen vermochten. Davon legt ein in vielen Gauen Deutschlands bekannter und verbreiteter Spottvers beredtes Zeugnis ab:

Im Osten kämpft das tapfre Heer,

Im Westen steht die Feuerwehr.

Solch' einer blödsinnigen Verhöhnung würden die Franzosen nie beistimmen; sie sind zu sehr überzeugt daß die Gegner, die sie vor sich haben, tapfere und tüchtige Leute sind. Aber in diesem beleidigenden Spruch machen die bürgerlichen Parteien, die Junker und die Panzerplattenfabrikanten ihrer bitteren Enttäuschung Luft, die ihnen die jetzige militärische Lage auf den zwe

Die Feldpost – a miniature newspaper dropped as a propaganda leaflet over troops in front-line positions in World War I. Although propaganda leaflets – dropped by both sides during the two world wars – are not really postal items, they are often collected by specialists in military material.

British colonies overprinted stamps "War Tax" or "War Stamp" during the First World War. Numerous examples are provided (especially in the French colonies) of stamps surcharged with a premium in aid of the Red Cross war charities. The Red Cross and other aid committees also provided special labels to identify mail sent free by prisoners of war. Stamps and seals are also found guaranteeing free delivery for soldiers' mail. The Spanish Civil War of 1936–39 produced a vast quantity of stamps, charity labels and tax stamps to raise funds and also to publicize the propaganda of the various belligerents involved.

Another form of war stamp consists of forgeries of enemy stamps for intelligence or espionage purposes. During the First World War the British forged German and Bavarian stamps and used them to frank propaganda leaflets scattered over German territory. It was too dangerous for agents to buy large quantities of stamps in the post office, so they were forged abroad. In 1940 the British resorted to the same practice, forging Vichy French stamps portraying Marshal Petain, as well as contemporary German and Italian stamps. At the same time the British forged German

ration-cards, official documents and even military despatches. Thousands of such counterfeits were dropped by aircraft over occupied Europe in an attempt to disrupt the Nazi war machine.

The wars also caused shortages of stamps, which led to various makeshift solutions. In September–October 1914 the Chamber of Commerce in Valenciennes issued its own stamps during a shortage of contemporary French stamps. In 1940 in Dunkirk and Coudekerque the Germans authorised the sending of private letters from July 1 to August 10, on condition that *Besetzes Gebiet Nordfrankreich* (Occupied district Northern France) was printed over the French stamp.

Various issues of stamps were made during the Second World War for the use of governments exiled in Britain. Poland, Yugoslavia, the Netherlands and Norway issued stamps in Britain, for use in army camps and on board ships which had escaped from Nazi control, and in many cases these stamps were subsequently used in the countries concerned after the liberation. By contrast, stamps were issued for the use of troops serving with the various national legions of the *Waffen SS*. Stamps were issued on behalf

of the Flemish and Walloon Legions by Belgium, the Danish Legion, and the French Charlemagne Division of the *Waffen SS*. The exact postal status of these stamps has been challenged, and it is now considered that they were produced mainly to raise funds for the "volunteers".

In Italy, supposedly on the initiative of King Victor Emmanuel III, stamps were issued during the Second World War with a decorative coupon attached. These coupons featured various aspects of the armed forces. Some of the best engravers in the country offered their services and the resulting engravings are much sought after by Italian collectors.

Finally there is a large group of semi-official stamps or franking labels, designed mainly to publicize particular regiments or military units. They have no postal value but are little masterpieces of engraving. These have been used for many years in Switzerland and a magnificent collection of them is housed in the Swiss Postal Museum in Berne.

Every war, every minor campaign, of the past 150 years has yielded its crop of interesting material for the postal historian and military collector. The fore-going has dealt in some detail with the arrangements for combatants in the two great world wars, but similar procedure has been adopted at other times, and also for garrisons serving overseas in times of peace. Covers bearing fieldpost cancellations and the cachets of individual formations, regiments or squadrons can be found for minor wars such as those in Korea (1950–53) and Suez (1956) or even from British troops on active service in Northern Ireland since 1969. An unusual mark of today may well become, in the future a valuable collector's item.

Other aspects of military mail which attract the attention of collectors include covers from the various peace-keeping forces, from the Swedish troops stationed in the Saar after the First World War, and the Dutch gendarmerie in Albania in 1913, to the Indian contingent in Indo-China in the 1950s or the Irish troops in the Congo a decade later. Mail from United Nations peace-keeping forces also bears special postmarks and cachets. Covers, cards, stamps and postmarks of the different national contingents in the International Brigades which fought in the Spanish Civil War (1936–39) are also highly prized nowadays.

Left: A cover bearing one of the special stamps raising funds for volunteers of the French Legion serving with the Waffen SS on the Eastern Front, 1943. For years it was forbidden in France to possess stamps or covers of the Charlemagne Legion of the Waffen SS, but this ban has now been relaxed.

The United Nations has had an interesting postal history since its formation at the end of the Second World War. Highly prized are covers from the temporary venues of the UN, in London, Paris and New York, before it acquired its permanent headquarters in 1950. Since 1951 distinctive stamps have been issued at the UN headquarters in New York, as well as by the European Office in Switzerland, while First Day Covers, slogan cancellations and meter marks add considerable interest. UN forces have been involved in peace-keeping roles in many parts of the world, and stamps, postmarks, cards and covers from these forces now form a distinct branch of postal history. Right: label from the first mail from the Norwegian UN emergency forces in Egypt, 10 December 1956. Below: part of a letter stamped by a stamp-cancelling machine (UN emergency force, Gaza, 6 May 1956). It was stamped "postage paid" on its arrival in Oslo on 10 May.

Special embossed envelopes were used for Valentines and Christmas greetings. This cover was carried by Swarts Dispatch, one of the many private despatch companies which flourished in the United States in the 1850s.

7

Miscellaneous aspects of the posts

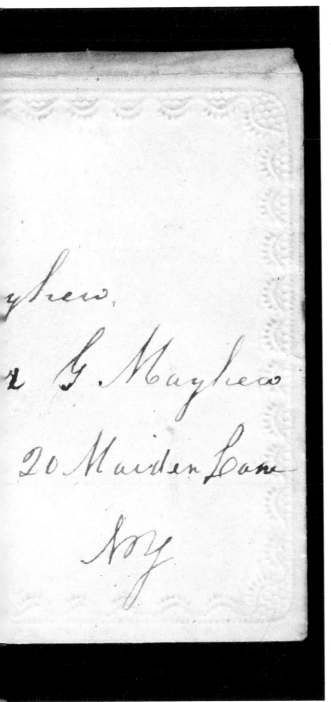

MANY collectors specialize in narrow areas of postal history, some rare, and some more accessible to the amateur philatelist. In this chapter we shall look at the origins of some of the material they collect.

LOCAL POSTS

In various places, at different times, throughout the world the official postal service has been unable or unwilling to provide a full service to the public. At these times it has been necessary for private organizations or individuals to assume responsibility for mail collection and delivery. These services are known as local posts.

One could fill a book with an account of these local posts alone, but it is sufficient here to cite a few typical examples. Mention has already been made, at the beginning of this book, of the existence of posts in ancient communities at a time when none was operated by the state (universities, merchants etc.). In addition, however, there were posts operating in restricted areas and at the disposal of the general public at times when a service was already functioning elsewhere. These were the forerunners of the local posts.

In eighteenth-century Europe delivery of letters from town to town was already well organized, but a letter posted for someone in the same town was apt to be discarded and never delivered. In 1680 William Dockwra, a London businessman decided he could profitably organize local deliveries, and he started a Penny Post in the cities of London and Westminster. (Some authorities attribute the origin of this service to a carpet-manufacturer named Robert Murray.) The Dockwra service flourished until it was suppressed following complaints by James, Duke of York (brother of Charles II, and later King James II) who felt that it infringed the monopoly which he, as head of the Royal Post, then held. The Dockwra service was subsequently absorbed into the government postal service. It is remembered on account of its excessively rare triangular postmarks.

We have already discussed the ill-fated post of

A
PENNY
Well Beſtowed,

Or a Brief Account of the *New Deſign* contrived for the
great Increaſe of *Trade*, and Eaſe of *Correspondence*, to
the great Advantage of the Inhabitants of all ſorts,
by Conveying of *LETTERS* or *PACQVETS* under
a Pound Weight, to and from all parts within the Cities
of *London* and *Weſtminſter*; and the Out Pariſhes within the
VVeekly Bills of *Mortality*,

For One Penny.

Here is nothing tends more to the increaſe of Trade and Buſineſs than a
Speedy, Cheap, and ſafe way of *Intelligence*, much being obſtructed
and more retarded in all Places where that is wanting. For as Money,
like the Blood in Natural Bodies, gives Life to Trade by its Circulation;
ſo Correspondence like the Vital Spirits, gives it Senſe and Motion:
and the more that theſe abound in any Place, the more doth that
Place increaſe in Riches, Strength, and Vigor.

But in this Age it is not to be expected that any New Deſign can
be contrived for the Publick Good, without meeting many raſh
Cenſures and Impediments, from the Fooliſh and Malicious; therefore 'twas not likely this ſhould eſcape that common Fate. Yet We
hope to all the reaſonable and Candid, who are willing to underſtand their own Intereſt, this
Paper may be Satisfactory.

For 'tis undertaken by the Methods of that Correspondency ſettled, that any Perſon may
promiſe himſelf his *Letter* or *Pacquet* ſhall ſafely come to any place directed to, lying
within the Cities and Suburbs of *London* and *VVeſtminſter*, and all their contiguous Buildings;
also to *VVapping*, *Ratcliffe*, *Lyme-houſe*, *Poplar* and *Blackwall*; to *Redriſſe*, *Southwark*,
and ſo to *Newington* and *Lambeth*; to *Hackney*, *Iſlington*; and all other places within the
Weekly Bills of *Mortality*, be it farther or nearer, to and from any of the aforeſaid Places,

For One Penny.

The times for iſſuing out of *Letters* to any of the aforeſaid Places, to be in the Summer time
from Six in the Morning to Nine at Night, and at reaſonable hours agreeable to the Winter Seaſon.

To the moſt remote Places *Letters* ſhall be ſent at leaſt Five times a day.

To Places of quick Negotiation within the City, and in the Term time for ſervice of the
Law Buſineſs, &c. at leaſt Fifteen times a day.

No *Letters* that come after Nine at Night, to be delivered till next Morning (except ſuch
Letters as are for the *Poſt-Office* General.)

By this means all Perſons, as well Gentlemen, Lawyers, Shop-keepers, and Handi-
crafts Men, that make and deal in Commodities vended by Patterns and poor Priſoners,
and all others, have that diſpatched for a *Penny*, which uſually coſts Three Pence, Six Pence, or
a Shilling. Now to oblige Men to pay more when they can hereby be cheaper ſerved, were to im-
poſe an illegal Tax upon the Inhabitants without their Conſents.

Beſides many Journeys of Taylors, Weavers, and other poor Artificers, and their Servants,
will be ſpared, who now conſume much time abroad in going to and fro, to the im-
poveriſhing of their Families, becauſe they cannot extravagantly pay a Porter for a Meſſage,

Renouard de Villayer with his carriage-paid service in Paris. A century later, in 1759, a philanthropist named Piarion de Chamousset instituted another *Petite Poste* (in opposition to the official *Grande Poste*) in Paris. Everything was provided for, down to the minutest details. The postmen had a uniform, complete with a hat and a "rattle", a wooden plate on which an iron knocker tapped to the right and left. 541 mailboxes were set up in shops throughout the city. They were emptied several times a day, and an ingenious scheme for sorting mail permitted several distributions of letters each day. This service also delivered announcements of births, marriages and deaths. Like Dockwra's Penny Post, it was a great success.

Other French towns, such as Marseilles, Lille, Lyons, Bordeaux and Nantes also had their *Petites Postes*. A series of slugs in the postmark gave details of the mailbox, postman and office so that delays and misrouting of letters could be avoided. In Lyons a special by-law forbade the postmen to use their rattles during the first round of the morning, so as not to disturb the ladies in their beds at that unearthly hour.

At Vienna a French emigré named Hardy organized a Little Post in 1772, charging postage according to the distance the letter was carried.

Left: An announcement concerning the establishment of the London Penny Post by William Dockwra in 1680.

A cover of 1766 bearing the distinctive triangular postmark invented by Dockwra and subsequently taken over by the Government post. The letters in the triangle are W (Westminster, the office of posting) and MO (Monday). The circular mark beside it shows the hour, 9 o'clock, and the letter T indicates that it was handled by the Temple post office.

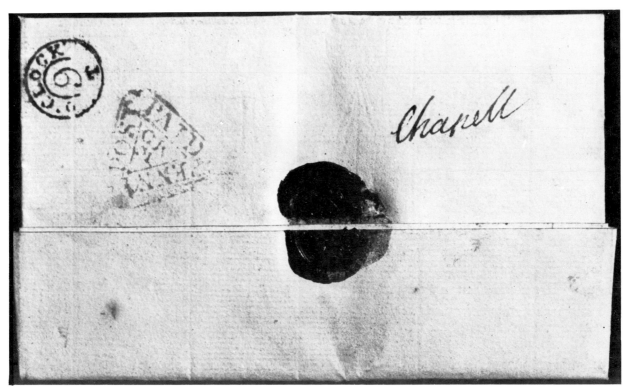

In Belgium another Frenchman, the Chevalier de Lespinard, proposed in 1776 to the Procurer General of Brabant the establishment of a local post at Brussels where local letters were not, at that time, distributed. His proposal was rejected by the authorities on the pretext that it would allow revolutionary tracts and other libellous material to be disseminated with impunity. Furthermore, they added that even if they had agreed to such a scheme, they would not have entrusted it to a foreigner!

House to house delivery was not instituted in the United States until 1863 and in the twenty years before that time numerous carriers and local despatch companies sprang up in virtually every city of the country. As most of them also issued their own stamps and postal stationery they provide a most interesting and colourful aspect of American philately. In Europe, private letter despatch companies flourished in the Scandinavian countries and also issued their own stamps. Local posts functioned in the Danish towns of Aalborg, Aarhus, Copenhagen, Fredericia, Odense and Osterroes, while the Norwegian local posts operated in Arendal, Bergen, Christianssund, Trondjhem, Hørten, Levanger and Tromso as well as Christiania (Oslo). In Sweden they were not so numerous, being confined to Göteborg, Malmo and Stockholm, while Finland had posts in Helsingfors, Tammerfors, Tavastehus and Bobaco.

In Germany, in the closing years of the nineteenth

A cover bearing the local stamp of Bouton's City Dispatch Post, portraying Zachary Taylor, twelfth President of the United States.

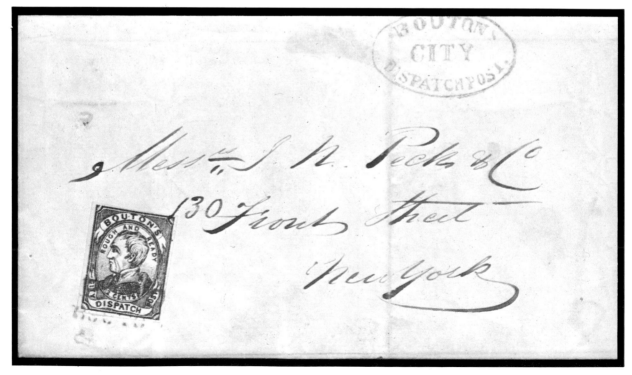

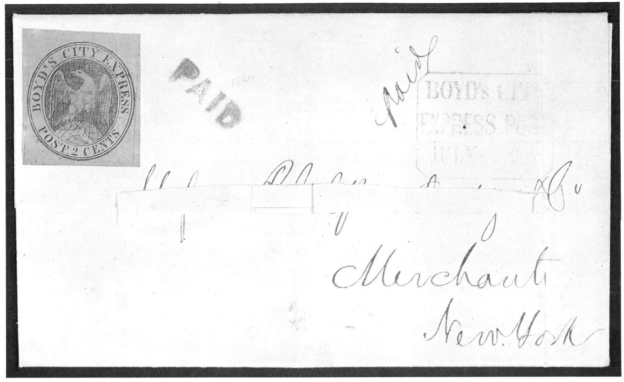

Another New York local cover, franked with the stamp of Boyd's City Express Post. Note the use of a FREE mark as a cancellation on the adhesive stamp.

A cover bearing the stamp of Carter's Fifth Street Despatch Post, Philadelphia, Pennsylvania, 1850. It also bears the mark of Briggs Despatch.

Following page: A local post was established in Paris in 1759, complete with uniformed postmen, and mailboxes. The boxes were emptied and deliveries made several times each day.

century, local posts were authorised in many towns and cities. These companies issued numerous stamps, postcards, envelopes and wrappers, many of them beautifully produced and designed. They include the world's first commemorative stamps, issued for the Ninth All-German Shooting Contest of 1887 (a year before New South Wales produced the world's first government sponsored commemorative stamps). Many of the postal services also issued mourning stamps following the death of Kaiser Wilhelm I and Kaiser Friedrich-Wilhelm, both in 1888.

In the immense empire of the Tsars the districts away from the great lines of communication were practically cut off from the rest of the country. Certain provincial assemblies therefore decided to organize local postal services in default of a state system. The first of these rival services were established at Schlüsselburg and Vetluga in 1865, followed by others at Verchnie (1866), Kozielets (1867), and Voronezh (1869). In the following year Baron Velhio, the Postmaster-General, decided to extend the system, provided there were certain guarantees, and a veritable charter for local postal services was published. Thus within each district, mail could be distributed by local postmen carrying mailbags embellished with the government coat of arms. (The posthorn emblem itself was reserved for the imperial service.) Local stamps had to differ in design and colour from those of the state, though a few are known

which closely resemble the government issues. Gradually the state accepted responsibility for several local postal services (82 from 1870 to 1900). About a hundred districts organized free postal services, subsidized by local rates and taxes; a further 170, in contrast, produced 2,427 types of special stamps. These served to establish the payment of the local tax, adding to the funds of the Russian postal service. These stamps are known to collectors as *zemstvos* from the Russian word for district. The stamps survived up to the time of the Revolution in 1917 and many **are still plentiful and cheap, though others are rare.**

In Switzerland in the last century the hotels in the mountain districts operated a postal service for their clients. An employee would take the mail to the nearest post office, often a difficult journey. The federal tariff was charged plus a tax of several centimes in favour of the hotel, usually denoted by special stamps. This practice was tolerated by the

Above, right: An interesting cover showing the *zemstvo* (local post) stamp of Bogorodsk used in conjunction with adhesive stamps of Great Britain.

Below, right: Several hotels in Egypt had their own post office. Perhaps the best known was Shepheard's in Cairo, which used attractive pictorial envelopes as a form of advertisement.

Adams and Co., forerunner of American Express, organized an express service between Boston and New York, using the Long Island steamboats. This cover bears the 50 cents stamp and was sent from Georgetown to New York by steamship, as the surcharge mark indicates.

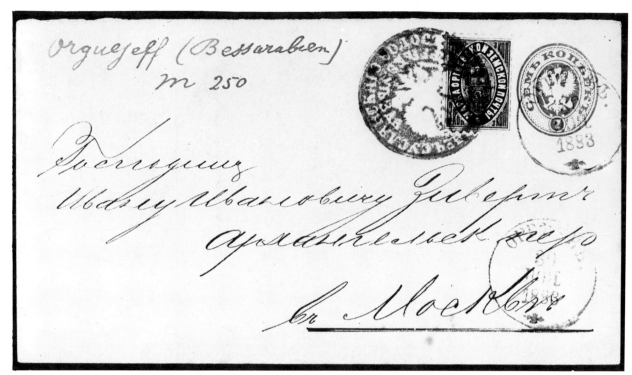

A cover bearing the stamp of Orgieff, one of the many towns in Tsarist Russia which organized its own *zemstvo* post.

A Rumanian stamped postcard, bearing the local stamp of the Hohe Rinne Hotel in the western Carpathians. The stamp celebrates the thirtieth anniversary of the hotel's local post.

federal authorities between 1844 and 1883. Some of these hotels were at a high altitude, like that of Bel Alp, on the southern flank of the Sparhorn at an altitude of 2,137 metres, the Rigi-Scheideck (1,607 metres) and Rigi-Kulm at nearly 1,800 metres. The stamps of the Swiss hotel posts featured mountain scenery and alpine flowers. A few hotel posts also flourished in Austria, the best known being the *Hohe Rinne* post in Transylvania

For a long time Morocco had no indigenous postal service, and it was left to various European businessmen to provide services linking the chief cities. The heyday of these Moroccan local posts was from 1880 till 1914. At the same time, of course, consular post offices were maintained in the chief ports by Britain, France, Spain and Germany. The local posts, with their numerous and attractive stamps, continued until October 1, 1913 when a Cherifian Post was established under the authority of the Sultan of Morocco. More than twenty services functioned around the turn of the century. In Madagascar and Constantinople, in the closing years of the nineteenth century, businessmen, often with consular backing, established postal services with distinctive stamps.

Other forms of local post have functioned in times of emergency: these are dealt with later in the book.

A Colombian express cover of the Tobon Company, from Buenaventura to Bogota, bearing the company's stamps.

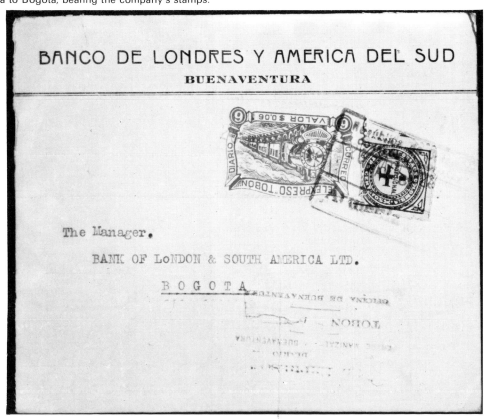

DISINFECTED MAIL

Over the centuries some very serious epidemics have ravaged the countries of Europe and Asia. Plague, yellow-fever, typhus, leprosy, cholera and small-pox caused millions of deaths in the era before the use of vaccines and serums. From 1789 till 1713 plague ravaged Denmark, Germany and Austria. In 1720 it broke out in the south of France, where it had not shown itself since the period 1629–49, and caused 8,000 deaths. In 1743 it appeared in southern Italy and in 1754 in Lisbon. These outbreaks, however, were nothing compared with the Black Death which swept Europe between 1346 and 1354 and caused over 24 million deaths. In 1665 London had lost 70,000 inhabitants while Milan a little earlier had lost over 150,000.

Plague was then incurable. All people could do was to try to protect their towns and countries by isolating them. Different measures were taken in ports and at frontiers, notably the introduction of quarantine for travellers and merchandise. Ships from suspect countries were immobilized in isolated yards until it was clear that they were not infected. Thus in 1788 a period of isolation of eighty days was observed in the case of plague. Travellers were confined in lazarets. These quarters consisted of bedrooms and other amenities (hospital, kitchen, wash-house, chapel, gardens) separated absolutely from the rest by an impassable "no man's land". Special fumigations were carried out to disinfect them. Merchandise was exposed to the air and the ships treated with lime from the hold to the between-decks.

Letters figured high on the danger list and they were treated in various different ways. Special postal establishments were often attached to the lazarets and quarantine stations for the fumigation of mail, and, in later times, these even had special postmarks. Letters were either slit with narrow cuts "to let out the pestilential air", or toasted over a sulphurous flame, or sprinkled with vinegar or some other disinfectant. Even gun-powder was used in some places. Eighteenth- and early nineteenth-century letters, with the tell-tale slits, scorch marks or stains

Right: The circular "Purifié au Lazaret Malte" (purified at the quarantine station, Malta) struck on a letter from the Middle East, 1838. Note the slits cut in the envelope to let out the "pestilential air".

A letter of 1839 from Turin to Furli (Roman States) bears an oval cachet with the words "Provincia de Bologna — Disinfettata" (Province of Bologna — Disinfected).

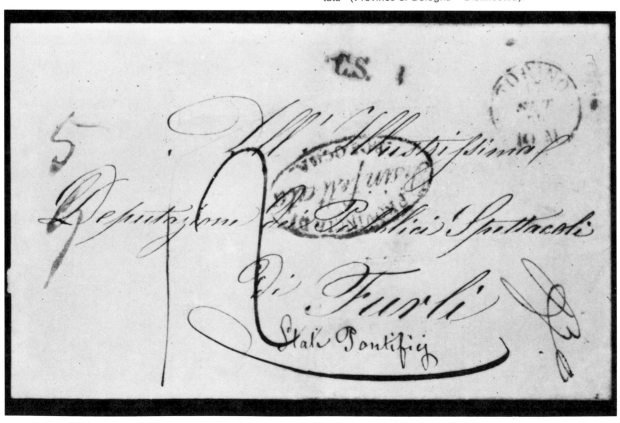

are of great interest to the postal historian, especially if they came from an area where the plague was known to be raging at that time. Europe was surrounded by a veritable cordon of quarantine stations stretching from the Black Sea to the Arctic Ocean. There were "sanitary boxes" at frontiers, and mail vans were equipped with sprays filled with sulphurous gas. They sprayed the outside of the boxes with the gas for up to six hours before it was considered safe to handle it. There were lazarets at Odessa, Constantinople, Alexandria, Malta, Semlin (Austria), Naples, Venice, Genoa, Marseilles, Toulon, Bordeaux, Spain, Hull, Antwerp, Hamburg, the Netherlands, Stettin, Kronstadt and Archangel among other ports, and the special cachets and postmarks which were struck on disinfected mail are highly prized by collectors. Some of these marks continued in use until the end of the nineteenth century, though the majority date from 1800 to 1850. These marks often bore such inscriptions as *Netto fuori e dentro* (clean both inside and outside), *Purifié au Lazaret* (purified at the lazaret) or *Geräuchert von Contumaz* (Fumigated from infection). In many instances special wax seals were applied to letters which had been opened out for fumigation and then closed again. The collection and study of disinfected mail is now regarded as a specialized branch of postal history.

MAILBOXES

A picturesque aspect of the posts is the many different types of mailboxes used all over the world. In the last century there existed on the high seas a kind of post office which was never manned nor subject to any control, but which operated a regular service. This "office" was established on one of the headlands of Patagonia which jutted out far into the middle of the Straits of Magellan. A large square stake was embedded in the rock and the words "Post Office" were daubed on it in red paint. From the stake hung a cask; passing ships called at this headland to pick up letters left in the cask and to deposit other letters which would be taken by the next ship going in the opposite direction. When they reached the next port, the letters were posted in the usual way. A similar arrangement operated at Cape Town in 1607, and at St. Helena a few years later, when East Indiamen collected or deposited letters under huge stones, known to this day as Post Office Stones. At Mossel Bay in South Africa an old shoe suspended from a tree near the shore served the same purpose, and this quaint practice is commemorated to this day by the special pictorial postmark of Mossel Bay which shows a "post office shoe".

At one time there were human letter-boxes in many large cities. In London, Paris and Vienna postmen

of the local post carried a sack or a box with an aperture in which passers-by "posted" their letters. These containers could only be opened by the post office. Later the boxes were fixed to walls or posts, and later became the self-standing pillar boxes so common nowadays. Post-boxes were also fixed to tram-cars and buses and in Germany and the Netherlands special postmarks were applied to mail posted in them.

The first six post-boxes erected in France appeared in Paris in 1653, in connection with de Villayer's Petite Poste. Before 1961 French mailboxes were painted blue, but since then they have been in yellow with a blue border. On Swedish mailboxes the word *Post* is inscribed over the royal crown and symbolic horn. In Switzerland the white cross on a red ground stands out clearly against the brilliant yellow background. In Denmark mail boxes are inscribed *Postbrevkasse*, while modern German mailboxes are most often made of glass-fibre strengthened plastic; a posthorn replaces the obsolete inscription *Postbriefkasten*. In Britain pillar boxes were introduced in the 1850s by Anthony Trollope, a postal official better known for his novels than his postal innovations. Since their inception, British pillar boxes have been painted bright red, though shortly before the Second War a few were painted light blue for airmail letters only. After independence the Republic of Ireland painted pillar boxes bright green. Since the 1950s Scottish pillar boxes have had a distinctive insignia, showing the Scottish crown without the royal monogram – Scottish nationalists objected to the Queen's title Elizabeth II (there having been no Elizabeth I of Scotland) and blew up pillar boxes bearing the offending monogram.

As an experimental measure, mail collected from pillar boxes was cancelled by special postmarks with a dotted circle in Dundee and Edinburgh in the 1850s, when such boxes were first introduced. Special postmarks to denote mail posted in a pillar box are used to this day in Australia.

THE FRANKING PRIVILEGE

At various times certain high personages, or those directly involved in state service, have had the privilege of sending their letters free through the post. Nowadays it is only the public services which benefit from this postal franking privilege. Among the exceptions to this are troops on active service, civil internees and prisoners of war, whose mail is normally permitted free of charge, often with special stamps or on specially provided cards.

In earlier centuries, however, the franking privilege

A Parisian post-box of 1850.

Left: A dotted circle cancellation was used in Edinburgh in the 1850s to distinguish mail posted in a pillar box. Pillar boxes were introduced to Britain in 1852.

was extended to many sections of the community. Religious orders, convents and abbeys, often enjoyed the privilege, a relic of their medieval exemptions from many of the secular taxes and charges of the state. Their letters could be distinguished by a special endorsement accompanied by a cross. This clerical privilege was often abused. All the inhabitants of a certain village in Burgundy, for example, were accustomed to send their letters in the name of the Superior of the abbey. He undertook to distribute the letters, charging a small tax. In France, under King Louis XV, the noblemen at the court were not content with sending their letters free, but despatched by post, game, poultry and fresh vegetables from their farms in the provinces. The struggle to curb such abuses was long and difficult.

Gradually a list of people entitled to frank their correspondence was drawn up and distributed to all post offices and from then onwards the postal service imposed successive restrictions. Each service was granted seals or stamps, which were rigidly controlled. The rights of the nobility were swept away at the Revolution, but the vast bureaucracy of the Directory, the Convention and ultimately the Napoleonic Empire carried on the age-old franking tradition.

In Britain, members of Parliament, both Lords and Commons, enjoyed the franking privilege, as well as the Royal Family, members of the Court and numerous national and civic dignitaries. Special postmarks, struck in red and inscribed FREE were applied to letters posted by these people. They had to endorse the lower left hand corner of their letters with their signatures. Many of these "franks" have been preserved by nineteenth-century autograph collectors. The franking privilege in Britain was abolished in 1840, when Uniform Penny Postage was adopted. Even Queen Victoria relinquished her rights, but they were revived by King Edward VII. Royal letters bear the monogram of the reigning monarch as well as a red "Official Paid" postmark.

In many countries the franking privilege of government departments was replaced by special adhesive stamps inscribed "Official" in their different languages. In Britain, contemporary postage stamps were overprinted with the names or initials of government departments. These stamps were not available to the general public but, following a leak to philatelists, they were withdrawn from use in 1904 and replaced by envelopes and postcards with an "Official Paid" stamp impressed on them. The familiar buff-coloured envelopes, "On His (or Her) Majesty's Service", have been in use ever since.

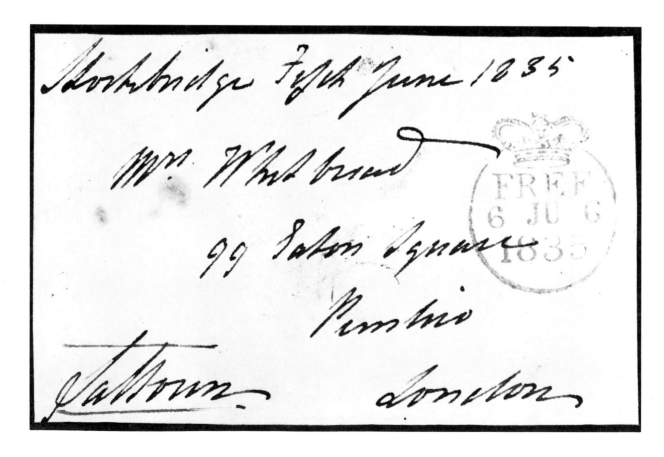

The United States likewise moved from a system in which government officials signed the envelopes to secure free postage, to issuing special stamps for each government department, in 1873. The stamps ranged in value from 1 to 90 cents and the same portraits of statesmen and celebrities appeared in each series. A different colour was used for each one: yellow for agriculture, carmine for the executive, violet for justice, red for the interior, blue for the navy, brown for the treasury, red-brown for war, green for the State and black on a coloured background for the post office. After a few years these stamps were discontinued and special envelopes and postcards are now used. These bear an inscription in the upper right hand corner setting out the penalty for improper use by unauthorised persons.

From time to time an individual has been accorded a franking privilege. In Spain in 1869 Don Diego Castell was allowed the privilege for his book *Cartilla Postal*, while Don Antonio Fernando Duro was granted it for his book *Resena historica de Correos* in 1881. At various times Portugal has authorised the

Civilian Marksmen Society, the Red Cross and the Anti-Tuberculosis Society to issue special stamps in order to frank their mail.

In many countries adhesive stamps perforated with an initial or initials are supplied to government departments. France gave the secretariat of the Senate authority to perforate its stamps with the letter S. In Germany before the Second World War the police used stamps perforated with a large P (*Polizei*). At one time the countless administrations of the numerous states in Germany used large circular labels with scalloped edges, usually with embossed designs, as a form of "seal" which franked their letters.

Similar labels, known as interpostal seals, were used in Egypt in the nineteenth century. Each Egyptian post office had its own distinctive seal, imprinted with its name. Some idea of the commercial importance of Egypt a century ago may be gained from the fact that these seals are found on covers addressed to Smyrna, Constantinople, Salonika, Beirut and Khartoum. The first series appeared in 1864 and was inscribed for the "European Post" which by virtue of a concession granted by the khedevial government ensured the postal service in Egypt. This enterprise was under the direction of an

Left: A British parliamentary frank of June 1835, autographed by Lord Saltoun.

Cover from Launceston, Tasmania to New South Wales, bearing the official paid frank of the Tasmanian Post Office.

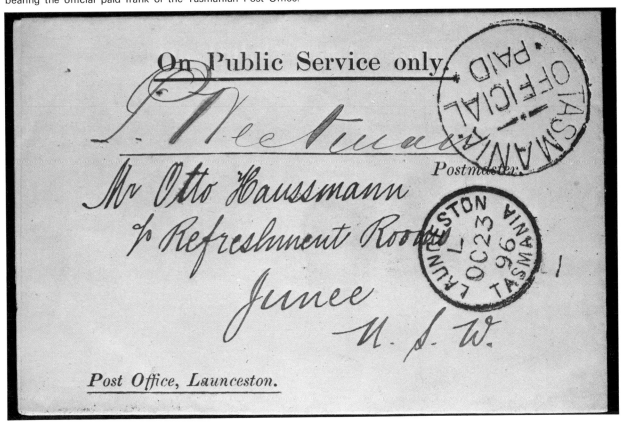

Letter carried by the Linz—Vienna emergency post during the Austrian rail strike of 1924. It was transmitted by road and posted on arrival in Vienna. Catholic charity labels were overprinted and used as stamps by this service.

A letter delivered during the British postal strike, 1971. Sent from Cook Island, New Zealand, it bears the special mail service surcharged stamp for the U.K. strike post, cachets of the philatelic bureau, Rarotonga and the Amsterdam transit office. It has a Dutch 45 cents stamp and is postmarked Amsterdam, whence it was brought by special courier to England in January, 1971.

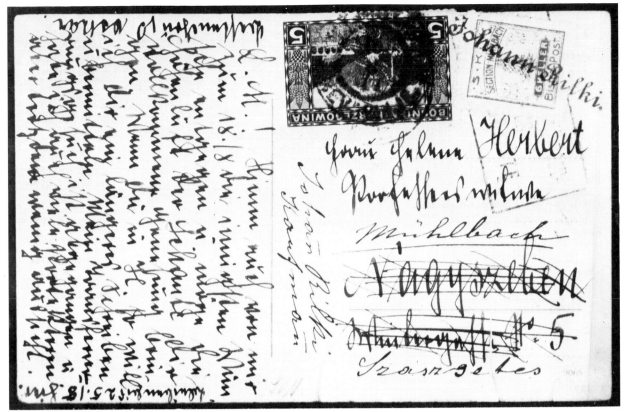

Postcard bearing a 6 heller Bistra local stamp, in combination with a stamp of Bosnia. The Bistra hotel in the southern Carpathians was formerly part of Hungary, but is now in Rumania. The hotel post came to an end at the outbreak of World War I.

Cover of 1878, bearing British stamps used in Beirut. Note the endorsement "via Brindisi"

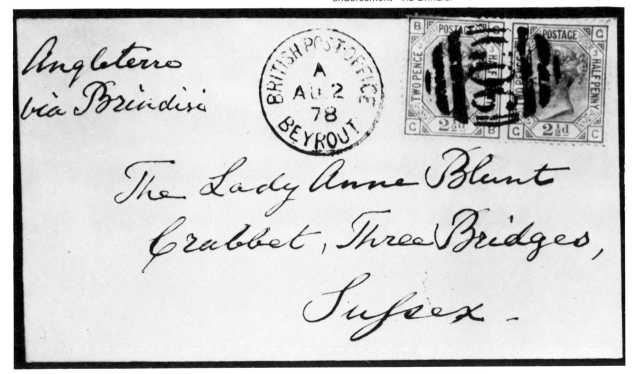

Italian, Giacomo Muzza, and the inscription found on the labels reflects its Italian origins: *Administrazione della Posta Europea in Egitto*, and later *Posta vice Reali Egiziane*. The Arabic text appeared in the centre. In 1877 control of the service passed to the Frenchman Alfred Caillard, under whose influence the inscription on the seals was altered to *Postes Egyptiennes*. Several hundred different interpostal seals have been recorded and examples are eagerly collected.

Communication between governments and their agents overseas is effected by means of special couriers whose task it is to carry the diplomatic bags. At the beginning of this century these bags were square and made of yellow leather, secured by a steel buckle and padlock. These cases are transported with absolute freedom through the customs and are immune to postal inspection. Naturally they contain reports, letters and printed matter, but quite bulky articles are often included as well. The use of diplomatic bags is suspended only in wartime. Mail sent by this means is often posted on arrival and bears the stamps or franking of the country of destination, even though the item may have originated thousands of miles away. Such diplomatic covers, often bearing the cachet of embassies and consulates in distant countries, usually bear the endorsement "By Bag".

EMERGENCY POSTS

From time to time exceptional circumstances have repercussions on the smooth running of the postal services and lead to items of unusual interest for the postal historian. The effects of war on the posts have already been dealt with, but civil commotion and strikes have also been known to disrupt services. Strikes by postal employees in particular have had a grave effect on the mails in recent years. Letters and parcels mount up and even after the strike is over there are considerable delays in clearing the backlog. The stoppage of mail during such strikes has a serious effect on commerce. In some cases troops have been called in to deal with these emergencies but usually it is left to private enterprise to provide a makeshift service.

On three occasions in one decade alone the British postal services have suffered delay or total breakdown due to industrial action by postal workers. In 1962 a strike led to the suspension of the letter mail for several days and a longer delay in the parcel service. Several bodies, of which the People's League for the Defence of Freedom was the most important, organized temporary services. The People's League even handled letters franked with their own markings,

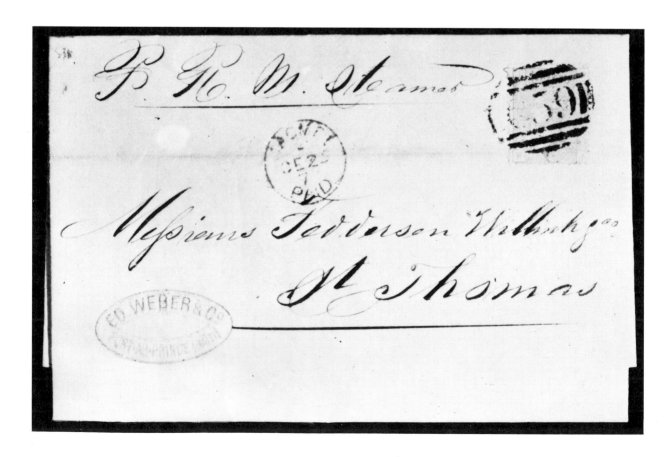

until the Postmaster-General stepped in and ordered the League to desist on the grounds that it was infringing a government monopoly. It continued to handle parcel mail, for which special stamps were produced. In April 1964 another pay dispute led to a postal "go-slow" and though the services continued to function, the situation soon became chaotic. Again the Freedom Group (of which the People's League was a part) stepped in and organized a parcel service, complete with special stamps. An interesting feature of covers at this time is that the time and date plugs were often removed from the cancelling machines so that the public would not be able to tell how long their letters had been delayed in the post!

The worst postal stoppage, however, occurred in January–February 1971. Anticipating a protracted struggle the Minister of Posts took the dramatic step of waiving his monopoly and permitting private carriers to handle letters and postcards as well as parcels, providing that they had authorisation from their local postmaster. As a result over 300 postal services sprang up overnight, from Glasgow to Dover and from the Isle of Man to the Isle of Wight. Significantly many of these services were operated by stamp dealers, with an eye to the main chance, and many of the services can be seen in retrospect to have existed solely for the purpose of allowing their promoters to produce as many different stamps as possible. The changeover to decimal currency in the middle of the emergency merely served to double the possible number of stamps issued!

A few of the larger companies, however, did offer a genuine service, and by the end of the emergency many of these companies had combined operations to provide a reasonably efficient network. Letters from the Isle of Wight to London might end up with the stamps of three different companies – providing an eye-catching memento of the crisis. Arrangements were also privately made for letters from abroad.

Strike posts have also functioned at various times in the United States, Canada, France and Italy. Emergency posts in time of war have been organized

Left: A cover of September 1872, bearing a British stamp postmarked at Jacmel, Haiti, and addressed to St. Thomas in the Danish West Indies. St. Thomas was an important centre for Caribbean trade and a port of call for ships plying between America and Europe, hence the large quantity of mail which bears the St. Thomas transit mark. The oval mark "Go. Webber and Co Port au Prince" is merely a tradesman's cachet.

A cover of March 1879, from Gibraltar to Italy. British stamps were used in Gibraltar until 1885.

by private enterprise. During the Commune, which followed the Siege of Paris in 1871 the city was cut off from the outside world. A company known as Moreau & Lorin handled letters and issued distinctive stamps for the purpose. In the First World War a Dutch organization handled mail between Belgium and northern France, both under German occupation. This service, operating from neutral Holland, handled British mail as well as French and Belgian correspondence. Leaflets gave details of how the address should be written, and of other regulations.

In August 1945, when the roads of France were pitted with bomb craters and lined with the wreckage of the defeated German army, a postal service by means of bicycles was organized between Nantes, Angers, Tours and Paris, while a similar network operated in the south of France. The youthful volunteers performed a speedy service thanks to relays and good co-ordination. The service lasted barely thirty days and examples of the covers carried in this way are very scarce.

Left: The Kingdom of Sardinia maintained a post office in Rome for much of the nineteenth century. This letter of 1843, to Trieste, bears the oval marking of the Royal Sardinian Consulate in Rome, the Rome date-stamp and the rectangular postmark of the Pontifical State (as Rome, under the temporal role of the Pope, was formerly known). On the back (below, left) is the crest of the consulate.

STAMPS USED ABROAD

For much of the nineteenth century, the postal services in the more backward, less developed countries were in the hands of foreign powers which had commercial interests in these areas. No fewer than twelve different countries maintained post offices in the Ottoman Empire, while Britain, France, Germany, Italy, Japan, Russia and the United States operated their own post offices in China at the turn of the century. Britain and France, however, had post offices and consular postal agencies all over the world and covers emanating from these remote places can only be identified by the appropriate numeral obliterator on ordinary British or French stamps of the period. Thus a British Penny Red with the numeral obliterator A 01 would have been used at Kingston, Jamaica, whereas one with the C 42 postmark would have come from Islay in Peru. Similarly a French stamp with the large figures 5080 would have come from Alexandria, Egypt.

A postcard bearing an Italian stamp overprinted for use at the Italian post office in Constantinople. No fewer than twelve countries maintained post offices in the former Turkish empire up to the outbreak of World War I.

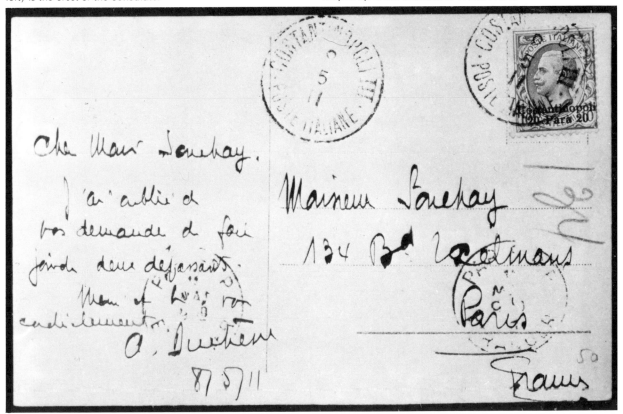

Maximum card of La Semeuse, Oscar Roty's famous design
for the French coins and stamps. This is not a true maximum
card in the strict sense, as although the card and the stamps
show the same picture, there is no matching postmark.

8
First day covers
and maximum cards

WITH THE growth of philately as a world-wide pursuit, certain aspects of postal history have been developed primarily to cater for collectors. The maximum card is now an important branch of philately in its own right and has been in existence for quite a long time. A maximum card may be defined as a picture postcard whose picture, adhesive postage stamp and postmark are all linked in some way. Maximum cards are now very popular all over the world. This hobby developed out of the craze for picture postcards which itself began in the closing years of the nineteenth century. At first it was sufficient for collectors to mail postcards from the places depicted on them. One often comes across, in old postcard albums, cards with the stamps affixed to the picture side so that when mounted in an album the stamp, postmark and picture are visible at the same time. Gradually, as stamps themselves became more pictorial, it became possible to get a stamp which was linked to both postmark and view on the postcard.

In more recent times many countries have begun the practice of using special or commemorative postmarks and these, used in conjunction with souvenir postcards of special events, have helped to popularize the maximum card. Finally, it is now usual for special postmarks to be produced in connection with new issues of stamps and quite a large industry has developed in the manufacture of special postcards whose subject is closely related to the stamp. In many cases the postcard features the identical subject used by the designer of the stamp.

To get maximum cards also required the co-operation of the postal administration, but unfortunately many authorities frowned on such irregularities as getting cards postmarked without then sending them through the post, cancelling stamps on unaddressed cards, or postmarking stamps placed anywhere other than on the address side of the card. However, bowing to popular demand, most post offices have now given way and maximum cards are permitted almost everywhere. Maximaphily, as it is

sometimes called, has now gone to the other extreme and little is now left to the ingenuity or individual tastes of the collector to assemble the criteria of a maximum card in his own way. This stereotyped, rather mechanical approach may detract from the popularity of theses cards.

SOUVENIR COVERS

Apart from first day covers and maximum cards, the collector will frequently encounter covers and cards bearing stamps with pictorial cancellations, cachets or decorative vignettes. These are produced for a wide variety of reasons, not necessarily connected with the first day of issue. All manner of events – fairs, exhibitions, state visits, political conferences, trade congresses and even the dedication of monuments and buildings, are celebrated philatelically in this manner. "Special event" covers, as these items are sometimes termed, form an interesting branch of postal history which is rapidly growing in importance and popularity. Though such material dates back as far as the Great Exhibition in London (1851) and the Centennial Exposition in Philadelphia (1876) the majority of covers and cards in this *genre* date from the beginning of this century.

FIRST DAY COVERS

Commercialization has also spoiled the hobby of first day cover collecting. Dealers and even postal agencies and philatelic bureaux now offer such comprehensive services that little remains for the philatelist to do but place a standing order and let the FDCs roll in. For those who like to take a little trouble, however, this is still a fascinating, and often rewarding hobby.

It all began early this century when collectors turned from unused stamps to collecting fine used specimens. At first they would mail a cover bearing a set of the new stamps on the day of issue, sending it to themselves and then soaking off the stamps on receipt of the cover. Gradually, however, the idea developed that stamps with a clearly dated postmark of the first day of issue were somehow more desirable, and such covers came to be studied and collected for their own sakes.

At first any ordinary envelope would do, but by the early 1920s, especially in the United States of America, dealers were selling specially prepared envelopes, decorated with an inscription and sometimes a vignette connected with the new issue of stamps. The idea spread to other countries and since

A souvenir postcard of the Leipzig Printing and Graphics Exhibition, 1914 — a very early example of a pictorial machine cancellation.

Above, left: A "maximum cover" from the United States, showing the Victory propaganda stamp of 1944, postmarked at the town of Victory, Vermont.

Right: A maximum card from the Turin Exhibition of 1928, bearing a stamp from the series marking the centenary of Emanuel Philibert, the tenth anniversary of victory in World War I. The postmark was applied at the exhibition itself.

A Japanese maximum card, depicting a montage of obsolete stamps in conjunction with the new issue and the pictorial handstamp.

Left: An American maximum card produced in 1932 to mark the bicentenary of the birth of George Washington. The special Washington stamp bears the postmark of Washington DC.

Right: A set of picture postcards portraying Napoleon, published to celebrate his centenary. The set consists of ten different cards, together making up a complete portrait. They were posted at an exhibition in Innsbrück – *La Croix Rouge et la Poste* (The Red Cross and the post), and are franked with special commemorative postmarks.

the Second World War the collecting of first day covers has developed enormously. The hobby was stimulated by the provision, in many countries, of special postmarks to cancel stamps on the first day of issue. In addition, many countries also publish special first day covers, which purists prefer to those produced by private stamp dealers. The special postmarks and covers connected with this branch of postal history may be recognized by such inscriptions as *Premier Jour d'Emission* (French), *Primo Giorno d'Emisione* (Italian), *Ersttagsbrief* (German) *Första Dagsbrev* (Swedish) or the equivalent in other languages.

In recent years First Day Covers have been used increasingly by commercial organizations for the purposes of advertisement, especially if there is a connection between the subject of the stamp and a particular commercial product. Even when the subject of the stamps has no connection, FDCs can still be used. The Medical Mailing organization sends out brochures on new drugs and medical equipment to doctors in Britain and other countries, enclosed in

First Day Covers. This ensures that the leaflets are not immediately thrown into the wastepaper basket, as they might otherwise be.

First day covers are nowadays commoner than ordinary commercial covers franked with the same stamps, and from the viewpoint of the investor this seems to defeat the object of the exercise. At least maximum cards may serve to instruct the collector regarding the subject matter of the stamp, or indicate the source from which the designer drew his inspiration. In a sense maximum cards add a new dimension to philately; they may instruct the philatelist and even improve his artistic taste.

Personally I recall how proud my younger brother, living in Russia in 1913, was of a series of postcards which he had, franked with the complete series of stamps marking the tercentenary of the Romanov dynasty, and including the celebrated five rouble stamp with the portrait of Tsar Nicholas II. I wonder where these cards are now. Have they survived? Or are they, like their illustrious subject, vanished for ever?

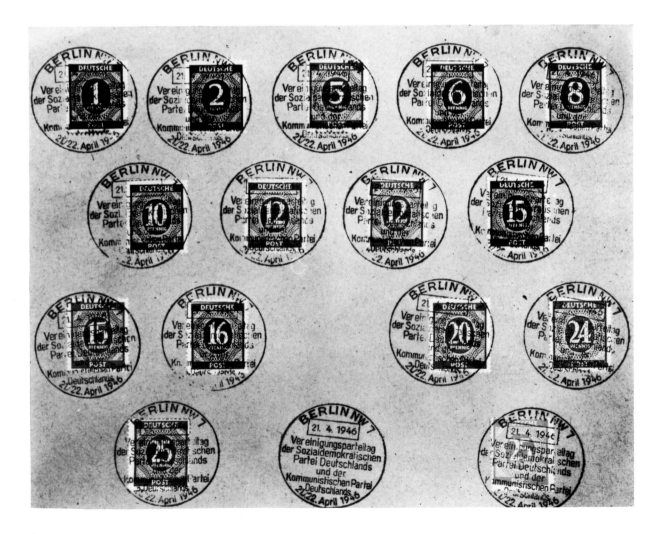

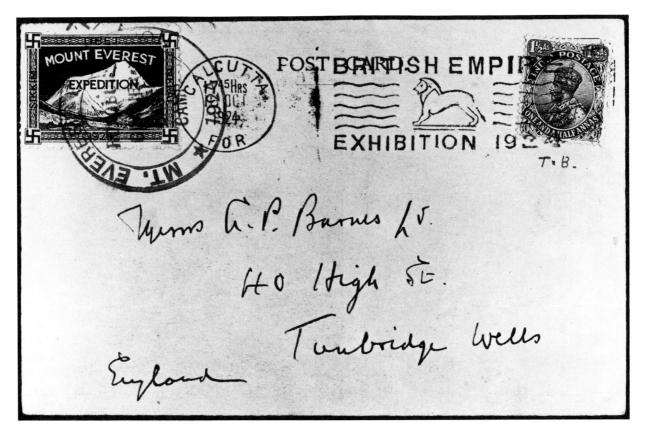

Cover bearing the special label of the 1924 Mount Everest
Exhibition. Note the slogan postmark, applied at Calcutta,
advertising the British Empire Exhibition at Wembley, 1924–25.

Left: A card bearing the definitive East German series of 1946,
cancelled with the special handstamp used at the conference
which resulted in the union of the Social Democrats and the
Communists to form the Socialist Unity Party of East Germany.

Right: Part of a souvenir card from the Nazi regime. The stamp
portrays Hitler and Mussolini and commemorates the latter's
visit to Berlin. The three pictorial postmarks portray Horst
Wessel, an early martyr of the Nazi struggle for power, clasped
hands symbolizing Italo-German solidarity, and a family
scene on the date-stamp used at the Goebbels *Heimstatte*
(institution).

A cover celebrating the twentieth anniversary of the Austrian Olympic Committee, bearing an Olympic meter mark, pictorial handstamp, commemorative airmail cachet and 10 schilling Olympic fund-raising label.

The centenary of stamps in Queensland, Australia, was celebrated with this first day cover.

In 1966 the World Cup Football championship was held in Britain. The stamp issued for the occasion is used on a Medical Mailing first day cover from Wembley, where the cup final was played. The British Post Office provides special postmarking facilities for Medical Mailing covers, and these are therefore of interest to specialist collectors.

COLLECTING COVERS AND CARDS

The scope for collecting is so vast that the would-be collector should have little problem in deciding what to study. His choice will be dictated by the availability of material and the size of his purse. At one extreme, the collector of modern slogan postmarks need never spend a penny on his hobby if he has access to the commercial mail of a large business firm. Many large mail-order companies, for example, will sell sacks of covers to collectors at little more than waste-paper salvage rates, and these are a fertile source for current postmarks. Earlier material is more elusive, but from time to time, with redevelopment of the business sections of large cities, large accumulations of old correspondence fall into the hands of waste-paper merchants and eventually trickle on to the philatelic market. Most stamp dealers and auctioneers now handle this sort of material, though the supply never keeps up with the growing demand. Dealers are also the main source for such material as first day covers, maximum cards and other items specially produced for sale to collectors, though the specialist collector would do well to contact the sales bureau of the postal administrations whose covers he intends to collect.

There are many ways of housing the collection. Special cover albums, with acetate or cellophane pockets, are now produced in Europe and America, but they are relatively expensive and as the collection grows rapidly the cost of buying more and more albums becomes a major problem. Standard, loose-leaf stamp albums are cheaper, but require the items to be affixed to the pages with photographic mounting corners. Always use corners with clear cellophane, never those with paper of various colours for these tend to be unsightly and detract from the items displayed. This system also permits the collector to annotate the page with the salient details of the covers and cards. Maps, diagrams of post-routes, photographs and press-cuttings can then be used to dress up the collection and add considerably to its interest.

For storage purposes stout cardboard boxes (large shoe boxes are admirable) can be used, and these have the merit that a bulky collection, running to thousands of covers or cards, can be stored neatly and take up a minimum of space.

A great deal can be done to improve the appearance of items, especially those which have lain in dusty archives for many years. Dirt marks can be removed with a soft artist's rubber or even with white bread-crumbs. File-creases can be removed by lightly applying a heated iron over brown paper on the affected cover. This requires great care since the paper can easily become scorched.

Rust marks, or foxing (a kind of fungus) can be removed by applying a weak solution of Chloramine-T to the affected parts, rinsing off carefully and then drying and pressing the cover between sheets of clean blotting paper. Chloramine-T, sold by chemists and drugstores in tablet form, should be dissolved in water in the ratio of ten to one, and painted on with a fine camel-hair brush.

Occasionally old covers may be encountered with doodling or other irrelevant ink-marks on them. To some extent ink removers and other bleaching agents will get rid of these unsightly marks, but again great care must be taken, for the remedy can be more harmful than the problem in the first place.

Where covers have interesting postmarks or cachets on both sides collectors are faced with a problem: either to leave the cover as it is, and display one side only when the item is mounted in the album; or to slit the sides and open out the cover to show both sides. Some collectors regard this as a form of vandalism; others regard it as perfectly permissible. The individual must make up his or her own mind on this point. A golden rule in postal history collecting is *never* to cut out a postmark from a cover without giving due thought to the result. Modern slogan postmarks, for example, are perfectly acceptable on pieces of envelopes, usually cut to the dimensions 10 by 5 centimetres. But remember, that once a piece has been cut out it can never be joined to the rest of the cover or card again. If an item has markings on both sides, or has an interesting vignette, or an unusual address, it is best preserved intact. Pieces of envelopes can usually be mounted with ordinary stamp hinges, but *never* use gummed tape – sellotape, Scotch tape or any other similar substance with a rubber base. This material is ideal for doing up parcels but has a distressing tendency to turn brown with age and spread a viscous stain over everything with which it comes into contact.

In collecting, there are various ways of tackling the subject. Some collectors specialize in airmails, military mail, mail carried by ships or locomotives or mail connected with an organization like the Red Cross or the United Nations. Others collect slogan postmarks of their own country or the whole world. Often, in view of the availability of material, it is advisable to start by collecting all the different post-marks of one's own city, county, province or country, but as the collection develops it may be necessary to specialize in one or more aspects. At any rate, this is a hobby where the scope is enormous, the rules are few and the interest and fascination unlimited.

Books for further reading

ALCOCK, R. C. and HOLLAND, F. C.: *British Postmarks*, Cheltenham (1960)
ANGUS, IAN: *Stamps, Posts and Postmarks*, Ward Lock, London (1973)
BOWIE, ARCHIBALD G.: *The Romance of the British Post Office*, Partridge, London (1897)
BROEKMAN, J. H.: *Het Interessante van Poststukken*, De Branding, Amsterdam (1964)
FORSTER, R. K.: *The Postmark on a Letter*, Chambers, London
    Postmark Collecting, Stanley Paul, London (1960)
GRAVESON, SAMUEL: *Penny Post Centenary*, Postal History Society, London (1940)
KAY, GEORGE: *Royal Mail*, Rockcliff, London (1951)
KELLY, CLYDE: *United States Postal Policy*, Appleton, New York (1932)
LERALLE, ANDRE: *ABC du Collectionneur de Marques Postales*, Yvert, Amiens (1944)
LOWE, ROBSON: *Encyclopedia of British Empire Postage Stamps*, London (1947–62)
MACKAY, JAMES: *Cover Collecting*, Collecta, London (1968)
    Airmails, 1870–1970, Batsford, London (1971)
    International Encyclopedia of Stamps (International Publishing Corporation) London (1971–2)
MURRAY, SIR EVELYN: *The Post Office*, Putnam, London (1927)
ROBERTSON, ALAN W.: *Maritime Postal History of British Isles, 1760 to Date*, A. W. Robertson, Pinner (1955)
ROBINSON, HOWARD: *Britain's Post Office*, London (1953)
    Carrying British Mails Overseas, Allen and Unwin, London (1964)
    History of the Post Office in New Zealand, Wellington (1964)
SCHENK, GUSTAV: *The Romance of the Postage Stamp*, Jonathan Cape, London (1962)
SIDEBOTTOM, J. E.: *The Overland Mail*, London (1948)
STAFF, FRANK: *Trans-Atlantic Mail*, London (1948)
STUDD, M. A.: *Paquebot and Ship Letter Cancellations*, London (1953)

Acknowledgements

Photographs and documents are reproduced by kind permission of the following:

Bundespostmuseum, Frankfurt am Main: 12, 17, 21, 104
Direction Générale des Postes de Norvège: 149
Het Nederlandse Postmuseum: 39, 42, 75 (top), 78, 102, 107
Prince Dimitry Kandaouroff: 6, 74 (bottom two), 103 (left), 105, 116 (bottom), 117 (top right), 118, 127 (bottom two), 128 (top), 138 (centre), 138 (bottom), 140, 141, 143 (top), 144, 146 (top), 147, 148, 160 (top), 174, 176, 177 (bottom), 178 (bottom), 179
James Mackay: 30, 34, 38, 40 (top right and bottom), 41, 43 (top), 44, 45, 46, 48 (bottom), 50 (top and bottom), 51 (top and bottom), 52, 53, 54, 55, 56 (centre and bottom), 61, 67, 68, 70, 71, 72, 74 (top), 75 (bottom), 76, 77, 87, 88 (bottom two), 90 (top right and left), 91, 95 (top right), 108 (bottom), 110, 111, 112 (centre and bottom), 113, 114, 115, 116 (top), 117 (bottom), 122, 125, 126, 127 (top), 128 (bottom left), 129, 134, 136 (bottom), 137, 138 (top), 139, 142, 143 (bottom), 145, 146 (bottom), 150, 153, 154, 155, 158, 159 (bottom), 160 (bottom), 161, 162, 163, 164, 166, 167, 168, 169, 170, 171, 172, 173, 177 (top), 178 (top), 180, 181, 182

The Mansell Collection: 14 (bottom left), 69
Mary Evans Picture Library: 14 (bottom right), 26, 27, 43 (bottom), 60, 82, 83 (top), 85, 93, 94, 124
Musée Postal, Belgium: 25 (bottom)
Musée Postal, France: 16, 24, 62, 95 (right), 121
Novosti Press Agency: 31, 90 (bottom), 117 (top left), 123, 159 (top)
Paul Popper: 58, 106
PTT Museum, Berne: 14 (top left), 22, 23, 25, (top), 28 (left), 28 (right), 32 (top right), 36, 37 (top), 80 (bottom), 83 (bottom), 84 (top), 86, 88 (top), 96, 99 (right), 120, 156
The Post Office: 8, 18, 19, 29, 32 (bottom), 37 (bottom), 40 (top left), 48 (top), 56 (top), 64, 65, 92, 95 (left), 101, 108 (top), 152, 165
Radio Times Hulton Picture Library: 20, 80 (top), 84 (bottom), 89, 98, 99 (left), 100 (bottom), 102 (right), 112 (top)
United States Information Service: 32 (top left)
United States Library of Congress: 109

Index

Numbers in italics refer to illustrations

A

Aachen, 87
Acapulco, 69
Adams & Co., *158*
Adams, Samuel, 67
Adrianople, 81
Acncas, *14*, 15
Aeschylus, 15
Afonso, Luis, 29
African Postal Union, 33
Airgraph system, 99
Aix en Provence, 64
Alaska, 93
Albany, 31, 61
Alcock and Brown Transatlantic flight, 110–11
Aleppo, 39, 73
Alexander I, Tsar, 30
Alexandria, 29, 69, 73, 74, 121, 164
Allahabad flight, 1911, 106
Alsace, 57
ambulants, 89
American Civil War, 85, 124–6
Amsterdam, *42*, *90*
Anglo-Boer War, *128*, *138*
Antibes, 64
Apollinaire Vases, 16–17
Arab-Israeli War, 74, *135*
Argentina, *52*
Army Post Offices, 128–34
Arrow, 87
Asahuerus, King, 13
Assyria, 14
Atlantic balloon, 101
Auckland, 99, *117*
Australia, 111, 165, *182*
Austria, 25, 27, *28*, 33, 45–6, 53, 57, 61, 74, 133, 162, *182*
aviation meetings, 105
Avignon, 19

B

Babylon, 14
Baghdad, 73, 111
Baikal, Lake, 89
Balkan Wars, *128*
balloon posts, *96*, *100*, 101–5, *102*, *103*
Baltimore, 31, *51*, 74
Barnes, 67
Barrows, Benjamin, 31
Basel, 86
Batavia, *38*
Bates, Barnabas, *56*
Baylard, M., 62–3
Belfast, 67
Belfort, 103
Belgium, 25, 33, 53, 57, 61, 63, 74, 86, *90* 94, 122, 149, 154, 173
Bell, Henry, 61
Bentinck, 74
Berlin, 57, 87, 144
Bermuda, *52*
Berne, *24*, *32*, 33, *120*
biblical references to posts, 13–14
bicycle posts, *95*
Billets de Port Payé, 43–4
Bishop, Colonel Sir Henry, 39, *40*
Bishop marks, 39–41

Bistra hotel post, *169*
Black Sea, 61, 69
Blanchard, 101
Blucher, 86
Bogorodsk, *159*
Boîte mobile, *67*
Bombay, 69, 73
Bordeaux, 17, 25
Boston, 31
Boules de Moulins, 62–3
Bouton's City Dispatch Post, *154*
Boxer Rebellion, *126–7*
Boyd's City Express Post, *155*
Brant, Sebastian, 22
Brazil, 33, *52*, 53
Breviary of Alaric, 18
Brighton, 82
Bristol, 79
Britain, 17, 22, 29, 33, 46–50, 52, 55, 57, 63, 73, 79, 82, 99, 133, 141, *146*, 148, *159*, 161 165, 166, *183*
Britannia, 68
British India, 53
Brussels–Malines Railway, 87
Brussels World's Fair, *117*
Buchanan, James, *51*
Buenos Aires, 66
Buffalo balloon, 101
Bulgaria, *123*
Burritt, Elihu, 57
Bushnell, 67
Butchers' Post, 18–19

C

Cadiz, 17
Cairo, 73, 74, 111, *159*
Calais, 21, 66, *67*, 68, 85
Calcutta, 74
Caledonian, 61
California, 93
Campbell, Duncan, 31
Canada, *31*, *47*, 66, 93, *113*, 171
Canal du Midi, 63
Canal posts, 63
Cape Breton, 77
Cape of Good Hope, 73
Carinthia, 46
Carta postale bollata, 45
Carter's Fifth Street Despatch Post, *155*
Catch me who can, 85
Cavallini, cavalotti, *44*, 45
censored mail, *137–8*, 141–4
Cette, 86
Ceylon, 53, 74
Chalmers, James, 45, 49
Chappe, Claude, 121
Charlemagne, 18
Charles I, King, 29
Charles II, King, 39, 151
Charles the Bold, 21
Charleston, 31
Charlotte Dundas, 61
Cheap Postage Association, 56
Cheltenham, 87
Cherifian Post, 161
Chicago, 89
Chile, *70*, *125*
China, 26, 35, 45
Christiania (Oslo), 41
civilian internees post, 134–7, *138*
clandestine posts, 138–41
Clarke, Latimer, 92–3
clay tablets, 13–14
Clermont, 61
Cluché, Abbé, 57
Clyde, Firth of, 61
Coalbrookdale, 85
Coblenz, 61
Cod-fishers post, 75–7

Coelho, Francisco, 29
Cologne, 61, 87, 144
Colombian airmails, 109–10
Columbus, Ohio, 105
Comet steamboat, 61
Compagnie Générale Transatlantique, 69
concentration camp posts, *137*
Concord mail coaches, 85
Concordia, 61
Confederation of the Rhine, 27
Constantinople, *46*, *68*, 73, 81, *173*
Cook Islands, *169*
cork cancellations, *54*, 68
Coronation Aerial Post, 106, *108*
Corunna, 66
Costa Rica, 33
Courrier de l'Europe, 66
crash covers, 111–13, *116*
Crevecoeur, St Jean de, 66
Cromwell, Oliver, 39
Cuba, 129
Cugnot, 85
Cunard, Samuel, 68
Curaçao, *143*
Curtiss 'Jenny', 106–9
Cyrus, 15

D

Dagron, M., 98–9
Dalni (Dairen), 89
Dalswinton Loch, 61
Danube, 61
Darby, Abraham, 81
Darlington, 86
Dayton, Ohio, 105
Delaware, 61
Delort, M., 63
Denis Papin, 63
Denmark, 18, 33, *37*, 82, *87*, 109, 154, 162
Deutschland, 74
Dieppe, 66
diligences, 82–5
diligences de l'eau, 63
diplomatic bags, 170
dirigible balloons, 103
disinfected mail, 161, *162–3*
Dockwra, William, 151, *153*
Dodogno, Ottavio, *28*
dog posts, *94*
Donau Dampfschiffahrt, 61
Dover, *37*, 66, 67
Drava, 61
Dublin, *50*, 72
Dundas, Henry, 61
Dutch East Indies, *111*

E

East India Company, *38*
Eckener, Dr., 104
Ecuador, 33, 110
Edinburgh, 59, 82, 165
Egarter, Konstanzia, 46
Egypt, 13–14, 33, *55*, 74, 167, 170
Eider Canal, 63
Elephant locomotive, 87
Elizabeth, Queen, 29
emergency posts, 170–3
England – see Britain
England–Australia flight, 1919, 111
entry marks, *90*
envelopes, 52

F

Faeroe Islands, *76*
Fairbanks, Richard, 31

Falmouth packets, 66
Feldpost, Die, 147
Fernando Noronha, *104*
Field Post Offices, 129, *128–34*
Fiji, *76*
Finely, James, 81
Finland, 53, 154
First Day Covers, 175, 176–80
First World War, 92, 93–4, 104, 110, 126, 129, 145–8, 173
Fitch, 61
floating safe, *74*
Florence, 19
Forth and Clyde Canal, 61
forwarding agents, 64–5
France, 20, 25, 27–8, 29, 33, 43, *44*, 53, 55, 57, 59, 63, 64, 66, 67, 69, 74, 77, 79, *80*, 82, *88*, 92, 94, 105, *133*, 138, 144, 148–9, 153, 161, 166, 171
Franco-Prussian War, 74, 101, 117, *124*, 126, 134, 138
Franking privilege, 165–70
Franklin, 67
Franklin, Benjamin, 31, *32*
Frederick III, Emperor, 24
Friedrichshafen, 104
Fuerth, 87
Fulda River, 60
Fulton, Robert, 61

G

Galitzin, Prince Alexander, 30
Gallatin, 101
Gambia River, *61*
Geneva, 28, 39, *141*
Genoa, 19, 26, 33, 64
Germany, 20, 25, 27, 33, 53, 55, 57, 66, 74, 81, 82, 104, 105, *114*, 122, 133, *134*, 138–9, 154, 158, 161, 162, 165, *180*
Gibraltar, 73, *171*
Gilbert and Ellice Islands, *76*
Girl Pat, 74
Glasgow, 20
glider mail, 113
Gouvier, Manuel de, 29
Great Barrier Pigeon Service Co., 99
Great Trunk Canal, 63
Greece, 15, 33
Greenland, *110*
Greenock, 67
Grevelle, M. le, 63
Guiana, 110
Gustavaus Adolphus, 36

H

Haiti, *54, 170*
Halifax, 68, 77
Hamburg, 53, 144, 164
Hanau 'hennchen', *17*
Hanseatic cities, 33
HAPAG, 69
Havana, 66
Hawaii, 33, *51*
Helensburgh, 61
helicopter mail, 113–17
Heligoland, 74
Helvetic Republic, 30
'Hen and Chickens', 95
Herodotus, *Histories* of, 15
Herrmann, Emmanuel, 53
Hill, Sir Rowland, 46–50, *56*, 87
Hindenburg airship, 104
Hohe Rinne, *160*
Holyhead, 67
Homem, Luis, 29
Hong Kong, 69
Hotel posts, 158–61

Hrozny, Bedrich, 15
Hudson River, 61
Hungary, 20, 33, 53, 57, 81, 117, 133

I

Ibero–American, Postal Union, 33
Ijstroom ship, *38*
India, 53, 74, *181*
India Letters, *67, 122*
Interpostal seals, 170
Ireland, *50, 72*
Italy, 19, 25, 28, 29, 33, 59, 64, 69, 82, 92, 122, 133, 144, 149, 171

J

Jamaica, *39*
James I, King, 29
Japan, *26*, 53, 89, 111, 133, *178*
Jean-Jacques, 67
Jefferies, 101
Jerusalem, 17
Julius III, Pope, 64
Jutland, 63

K

Kafr Zayat, 74
Karoly, Akin, 53
Kayan Gorge, 61
Kidderminster, 46
Killingworth Collieries, 86
King, Archer, 101
Kingston, 67
Kitty Hawk, 105
Klagenfurt, 46
KLM airline, 111
Knight, Charles, 45
Korrespondenzkarte, 53
Koschier (Kosir), Laurenc, 46
Krebs, 103
Kun, Bela, *112*

L

Lady McLeod, 61
Lafayette, Marquis de, 67
Laibach (Ljubljana), 45
Lancrey, Pierre de, 31
Landes, 94, *95*
Le Matin, 57
Le Havre, 21, 65, 67
League of Universal Brotherhood, 57
Leeward Islands, 67
Leipzig–Dresden Railway, 87
Leipzig, 177
Leningrad, *118*
Lerici, 64
Lesseps, Ferdinand de, 74
letter cards, 53
Lichfield, Earl of, 49
Lilienthal, Otto, 105
Lisbon, 28, 33, 73
Liverpool, 68
Local posts, 151–61
Locomotion No 1, 86
London, 17, 29, 41, 48–50, 57, 59, 66, 69, 73, 74, 82, 85, 87, *92*, 104, 151, 153, 162, 164, 171
Lorient, 66
Los Angeles, *109*
Louis, XIV, 43, 63
Lufthansa, 111
Luxembourg, 33, 57
Lyons, 28, 74, 86

M

Maberley, Colonel, 49
MacAdam, John L., 79
Madrid, 66
Mahmoudieh Canal, 73
mail-boxes, 164–5
mail-coaches, 79–81
Mainz, 61, *163*
malles-poste, 82
Malta, 74, 164
Maly, Baron A., 53
manuscript endorsements, 37–9
maritime mail, 64–75
maritime postage stamps, 74–5
Marotiri Copper Syndicate, 99
Marseilles, *27*, 57, 65, 66, 67, *68*, 69, 74, 153
Massachusetts, 31, 57
Mata Coronel, 29
Mauritius, 53, 67, *72*
Maximilian, Emperor, 25, *28*
maximum cards, 175–6
Medical Mailing Co., 180, *182*
Mediterranean Sea, 69, 74
Melbourne, Lord, 49
Merchant Adventures, 29, 65–6
merchants' posts, 18–9, 59–60
Mesopotamia, 59, *113*
Messageries Maritimes, 69
Metz, 103
Metzer Post, 18–19
Mexico, 53, 65, 75
Milan, 19, 21, 39
military posts, 119–30
Miller, Max, 108–9
Miller, Patrick, 61
Millstadt, 46
Mississippi, 61
Missouri, 101
Monaco, 64
monastic posts, 19–21, *21*
Mont Cenis, 81
Montevideo, 66
Montgolfier Brothers, 101
Montpellier, 86
Morehouse Martens Co., 105
Moscow, 30, 87
Moulins, 63
Moveable Box, *67*
Mulready envelopes, *34, 48*, 49–50, 52
Munich, 81
municipal posts, 22, *22*
Muzza, Giacomo, 170

N

Nagasaki, 89
Nantes, 105
Naples, 65, 121
Napoleon, 25–6, 81, 119, 141, *179*
Napoleon, 67
Nashville, 101
Nederlander, 61
Netherlands, 25, 33, 57, 61, 81, *83*, *114*, 122, 148, 164, 173
Newfoundland, 53, 111–12
New Jersey, 65
New London, 74
New Orleans, 65
New South Wales, 45, 53, 158
newspaper bands, 53
New York, 31, 61, 65, 66, 77, 89, 101, 106, 107
New Zealand, *41*, 99, *168*
Nice, 28, 45
Nile, River, 36, 59, 73–4
Norddeutscher Lloyd, 69
Normand, M., 68
North Sydney, 77
Norway, 33, *85, 87*

Nova Scotia, 77
Nuremberg, *22*

O

Ocean Penny Postage, 57
official mail, 166–70
Ohio, 41, *58*, 61
Old Down, 79
Ontario, Lake, 101
Oregon and California Steamship Co., 69
Orleans, 74
Oslo, 41
Ostend, 65, 74
overland mails, *71*, 73–4, *84*

P

Pacific Mail Steamship Co., 69
Pacific Steam Navigation Co., 68–9
Pacific Steamship Co., 69
Panama, 69
Panama Canal, 63
papillons de Metz, 103
Papin, Denis, 60
papyrus, 35
parachute mail, 117
parchment letters, 35
Paris, 21, *27*, 43, 55, 57, 61, 74, 82, 87, *90*, 92,
   101, 122, *156, 165*
Paris Postal Conference, *32*, 33
Paris, Siege of, 62–3, *96*, 97–9, 101–3, 173
   Treaty of, 75
patriotic covers, *131*
Paucton, 67
Pavlovsk, 87
Peninsular & Orient, 68, 73
Penny Black, *50*
Penny Red, *50*
Peoples League Post, 170–1
Perkins, Bacon and Petch, 49–50
Perot, William B., *52*
Persia, 14
Peru, *60*, *125*
Peter the Great, 30
Peutinger Tables, *16*, 17
Philip the Fair, 21
Piedmont, 28, 29, 64
pigeon posts, 97–9
pillar boxes, 164
Pinedo, Francisco de, 111, *112*
pneumatic posts, 57, *92*
Poland, *131*, *138–9*
Pollard, James, 82
Polybus, 16
Pony Express, 93
Portugal, 28, 33, 82, *130*, 144
postal markings, 36–9
   propaganda, *56*, 57
   rates, 41
   stamps, 41–3, 49–50
   stationery, 52–7
   strikes, 170–1
post boats, 13
Post Circular, The, 49
Precursor, 74
prisoner-of-war mail, 130–4, *130, 136, 138,*
   142
   propaganda leaflets, *147*, 148
Prussia, *18*, 33
Prussian-Rhenish Steamship Co., 41

Q

Quebec, 31
Quester, Matthew de, 29

R

railways, 85–92
Rainham and Morgan Transatlantic flight,
   112
Rampont, Gabriel, 63
Red Cross, 6, 57, *127, 128, 130,* 134, *135,*
   141, 143, 148, 167, *179,* 183
Red Sea, 74
Renard, 103
Returned Letter Office, *10*
Reunion, 67
Rhine, Confederation of the, 25–6
Riquet, Paul, 63
river posts, 59
Roanne, 74
Robert, M., 63
Rob Roy steamship, 67
rocket posts, *116*, 117
Rocky Mountains, 93
Romans, *12*, 16–19, 36, 59
Rome, 16, 17, 19, 33, 39, 57, 64, 111, *172*
Rotterdam, *42*
Roty, Oscar, *174*
Rouen, 63, 87
Rumania, 33, *140, 169*
Royal Mail Steam Packet Co., 68
royal posts, 22–4, *24*
Rozier, Pilatre de, 101
Rudolph II, Emperor, 19
Russell, Major, 93
Russia, 30, *31,* 33, 61, 63, *82, 83,* 89, *117,*
   133, *135,* 144, 158, 180
Russian Refugee Post, *146*
Russo-Japanese War, 89, 92, *127*
Russo-Turkish War, *123*

S

Saint Etienne, 86
Saint Germain, 86
Saint Joseph, 93
Saint Lawrence, Gulf of, 77
Saint Pierre and Miquelon, 75–7
Saint Petersburg, 30, 87, 122
Saint Victor, Castillon de, 62
Saint Vital, Roll of, 21
San Francisco, 69
Santos Dumont, Alberto, 103
Sardinia, 44–5, *172*
Sauvage, Frederick, 67
Sava, 61
Savoy, 28, 45, 64
Scaramuccia, 28
Scotland, 45
Sea Post Office, *71*
Seals, 35
Second World War, 74, 99, 167
Seguin Brothers, 86
Seine, River, 61
Serbia, 33
Shanghai, 69, 89, 92
Ship Letter marks, *72*
Ship postmarks, *77*
Siberia, 81
siege mail, 62–3, 97–9, 101–3, 121
Simplon Pass, 81
sledge posts, 93
Smith, Adam, 59
Smith, F. P., 67
sorting carriages, *86*
South Africa, *76, 114*
South American Postal Union, 33
souvenir covers, 176
Spain, 18, 25, 33, 66, 82, *129,* 144, 167
Spanish Civil War, 74, *145*
Stanhope, Lord, 29
Stephenson, George, 86
stilt post, 94, *95*
Stockton, 21, 57, 86

Straunge Foot Post, A, 29
strike posts, 168, *168*
Stringfellow, 105
submarine posts, 74
Suez Canal, 73–4, 75, *136*
Suez Canal Co., 63, 74–5
Swarts Dispatch, *150*
Sweden, 33, 36, 45, 66, 82, 154
Switzerland, 26, 30, 35, 57, *80,* 82, 134, 149,
   158–61, 165
Sydney, 45, 69
Syria, 14

T

talismanic inscriptions, 37, *38*
Taxter, 67
Tel el Amarna, 13
telegraphs, 15–16, 121–6
Telford, Thomas, 81
Termonde, 87
Theodoric, 18
Thomson, John, 49
Thurn and Taxis, 24–7, *25,* 79
Tin Can Mail, 75
Tisza, River, 61
Tobon Co., *161*
"Too Late" marks, *47*
Tours, 97
Traclet, Lafollye, Tasiers and Blaise, 98
Trans-Siberian Railway, 89
Travelling Post Offices, *61,* 87–91
Treffenberg, Curry Gabriel, 45
Trenton, 61
Trevithick, Richard, 85
Trieste, 74
Trinidad, 61
Tristan da Cunha, *76*
Tsarskoe Selo, 87
Turin, *162, 177*
Turkey, 14, 33, 55, 69, 133
Tuscan posts in Rome, 39
Twyford, 87

U

Uniform Fourpenny Post, 49
Uniform Penny Post, 49, 166
United Nations, 33, *149*
United States of America, 31–3, 53, *58,* 66,
   67, 74, 87–9, 91, 99, 106–9, 113, 117, 130,
   144, 154, 167, 171
Universal Postal Union, 33, 55, 75, *91*
university posts, 20
used abroad, stamps, *169–70*

V

valentines, *150*
Valparaiso, 69
Vancouver Island, 69
Venetian Republic, 22, 43
Venice, 19, 28, 65
Versailles, 93
   Treaty of, 27, 67
Vicarello, Goblets of, 16
Victoria, Queen, 50
Vienna, 17, 21, 26, 33, 45, 57, 81, 113, 121,
   153, 164, *168*
Villayer, Renouard de, 43–4, 151–3, 165
Vinci, Leonardo da, 39
Vladivostok, 92
V-mail, 99
Vonoven, M., 63

W

Waghorn, Thomas, 74
Walkers of Rotherham, 81
war stamps, 144–9, *144–9*
Warsaw Ghetto, *138*
 Rising, *139*
Washington, 33, 106, 107
 George, 101, *178*
watermarks, 53
Watt, James, 60–1
Wellington, *41*
Wells Fargo, 93
Werder, General, 57
White Nile T.P.O., *90*
Wiener Neustadt, 53

William the Conqueror, 21
Windward Islands, 67
Wise, John, 101
Wolff Agency, 74
Wolowski, Louis, 55
Wrangel, Baron von, *146*
wrappers, 53
wreck covers, 75
Wright Brothers, 105, *115*
Württemberg, *90, 91*
Wyon, William, *50*

X

Xenophon, 14

Y

Yenisei, River, 89
Yugoslavia, 46, *142, 146*

Z

zemstvos, 158–61, *159, 160*
Zeppelin, Count Ferdinand von, 103–4
zeppelins, 103–5, *106*
Zucker, Gerhard, *116*